D1322001

Your Child's Body Language

By the same author:

Sibling Rivalry
Starting School

Your Child's Body Language

Dr Richard Woolfson

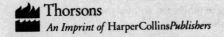

Thorsons
An Imprint of HarperCollins*Publishers*

Thorsons
An Imprint of HarperCollins*Publishers*
77–85 Fulham Palace Road,
Hammersmith, London W6 8JB
1160 Battery Street,
San Francisco, California 94111–1213

Published by Thorsons 1996

10 9 8 7 6 5 4 3 2 1

Text illustrations by Stuart Trotter

A catalogue record for this book
is available from the British Library

ISBN 0 7225 3185 0

Printed in Great Britain by
Caledonian International Book Manufacturing Ltd, Glasgow

To Lisa, my best friend

Contents

Acknowledgements

Thanks to Wanda Whiteley for help in preparing the final manuscript, and to Lisa, Tessa and Eve for their love and encouragement.

Introduction

You and your child read each other's body language all the time, though the chances are you don't realize that this non-verbal communication is going on. Yet interpreting body language is a vital part of every parent-child relationship.

Think about it for a moment: Have you ever smiled at your child? Of course you have – this means you've used non-verbal communication to express your feelings of pleasure to your child. Have you ever snuggled up close to your child, perhaps sitting with him on your knee as you read or watch television together? Of course you have – this means you've used non-verbal communication to express your feelings of love and closeness to your child. Have you ever stood very close to your child, almost face to face, as you've reprimanded him for misbehaving? Of course you have – this means you've used non-verbal communication to express your displeasure or anger to your child. These are only a few of the many instances when you use body language – deliberately or involuntarily – to 'talk' to your child.

And your child 'talks' to you nonverbally, as well. Has he ever cried? Of course he has – this means he has used non-verbal communication to tell you about his feelings of hunger, boredom, anger, discomfort, etc. Has he ever pushed his food away when sitting at the dinner table? Of course he has – this means he has used non-verbal communication to tell you that he doesn't want to finish his meal. Has he ever tried to hide behind you when someone he doesn't know tries to speak to him? Of course he has – this means he has used non-verbal communication to tell you that he's feeling shy. These are only a few of the many instances when your child uses body language – deliberately or involuntarily – to 'talk' to you.

Some psychologists claim that body language is more important than spoken language. Several reasons are given to support this belief. First, the amount of spoken language that is used in comparison to the amount of body language. One substantial research project concluded that, in a typical relationship, only seven per cent of what someone is feeling is expressed in words – 93 per cent of all emotions are expressed using a variety of non-verbal communication channels. Figures like this certainly put a new perspective on the importance of body language! If you can't understand your child's body language, then you will miss over 90 per cent of the thoughts and feelings he is trying to convey to you. You wouldn't be too pleased if the people close to you understood only 10 per cent of what you were trying to express – so your child won't be pleased if this happens in your relationship with him.

Second, body language is more dynamic than spoken language. Psychologists claim that, for every communication between two people, over 55 per cent of the meaning is conveyed non-verbally. One psychologist estimated the amount of body language between two people and concluded that the average person speaks for fewer than 20 minutes per day, and that the average sentence lasts fewer than five seconds! Most young children use words to communicate facts ('I need the toilet' or 'I'm tired'), and use body language mainly to communicate emotions (crying or frowning if they are unhappy; scowling if they are angry with someone). Understanding these non-verbal cues is a critical part of responding appropriately to your child.

The third reason for attributing so much significance to non-verbal communication in a parent-child relationship is the undoubted fact that body language 'leaks'. In other words, body language often reveals our true feelings, underneath what we express in words. Suppose you were going for a job interview, and that you were quite nervous about it. You wouldn't want this to show during the interview, so you might decide to speak slowly when asked a question, and to choose your words very carefully; you might even practise speaking without 'ems' and 'ers' punctuating your speech. In this way you would try to control your spoken language to hide your true feelings of nervousness. Nevertheless, your body language would give the game away, because it is much harder to control. Your breathing might become short and shallow, you might start swallowing a lot, you might have difficulty smiling even when the interviewer cracks a joke, your hands might be clasped tightly, your neck and head muscles might be very tight (resulting in a posture that is unnaturally stiff), or you might shift your feet too often. To put it simply, your true nervousness would show through non-verbally and there'd be little you could do about it.

The same applies to your child. Suppose you ask him if he drew the crayon mark on the living room wall. Although his first reaction might be to deny the incident because it was an accident and he doesn't want to be in hot water over it, you might be able to detect straight away that he is not telling the truth. He might, for instance, not be able to look you straight in the eye, or his cheeks might become flushed. These revealing signals let you know that there is a difference between what your child is telling you verbally and what he is telling you non-verbally. Where there is a conflict in communication like this, always be guided by the non-verbal message.

In addition, body language is often much more convincing than verbal language. An action *can* speak louder than words. A reassuring cuddle can be more supportive than a reassuring phrase; a smile and a thumbs-up sign can be more inspiring than words of encouragement; and a disapproving frown can be more effective than a verbal reprimand.

There are occasions when your child's body language gives you advance warning of a potential crisis, which allows you to take a preventative course of action. For instance, his sluggishness when putting his jacket on may tell you that he's reluctant to go to nursery; perhaps there is a problem there that you need to help him solve. It's easier for your child to express his feelings this way than it is for him to verbalize the true reason for his unhappiness.

Lastly, understanding your child's body language will strengthen your relationship with him. It stands to reason that the more you can understand your child, the closer you'll be to him. When parents fail to grasp what their child says to them – verbally or non-verbally – then frustration, even anger, develops as a result. The struggle to make sense of non-verbal communication can upset parents and children. Women suffering from post-natal depression, for example, often report that they can't tell what it is their baby wants from them, and feel unable to cope as a result. Good communication helps parents and children to feel more confident and to develop a deeper and stronger relationship.

Your Child's Body Language takes a practical (and sometimes playful) look at the different channels of non-verbal communication used by your child, and how each plays its part in his relationship with you. You'll learn how to sharpen your ability to read your child's body language, and the typical messages conveyed at each age and stage of development. Interpretation of your child's body language to detect when things go wrong in his life is considered. There is also advice on how to encourage your child to use body language more positively in his interactions with other children. All this will help you to be a more aware and effective parent.

Part One

Making a Start

Chapter One

Tuning in to Your Child's Body Language

Getting Started

There's no great secret about understanding your child's non-verbal communication – you just need to be observant and to know what to look for. Although you unconsciously read your child's body language anyway (for instance, when you see her crying or laughing, smiling or frowning, sulking or exuberant), there will still be a lot of non-verbal signals that you miss because they are not so obvious (for instance, shallow or deep breathing, back straight or shoulders hunched). And that's why you need to get 'tuned in' to body language. All it needs is a little bit of practice.

Key Skills

The chart below lists the key skills you need to interpret your child's body language accurately and perceptively.

Key Skill	Significance
Knowledge	Understanding body language requires good background knowledge of the major components of non-verbal communication and how they are commonly used by children. You already know a lot about this, but your basic knowledge of body language can probably be improved.
Observation	You won't be able to interpret your child's body language until you have the ability to look closely at her gestures. The more you know someone, the more you take her for granted – so get used to spending more time actually observing what your child is doing.
Openness	It's only natural to judge the meaning of your child's actions on the basis of your previous knowledge of her. However, these preconceived ideas can limit your interpretation of her behaviour. Be open to the notion that the meaning of her body language could surprise you.
Verification	There is no magic to understanding body language. The only way to be sure that your interpretations are accurate is to verify them objectively, perhaps by asking your child.

	Tell her what you think her body language means, and then ask her if she thinks you are right.
Flexibility	The study of non-verbal communication is not an exact science. Later in this chapter you will read how the same action can have different meanings depending on the circumstances. Therefore, you have to be flexible when interpreting your child's body language.

Practical Exercises

Here are some short observation exercises to help you sharpen these key skills. These brief activities provide a fun way of honing your perceptiveness.

In each of these exercises you will have to look closely at the people involved and make judgements about their thoughts, emotions and behaviour. Since you will be looking, not listening, you will have to base your assessment on body language signals alone.

During your observation, write down what each person 'says' with his or her body language and what feature of non-verbal communication was used to 'say' it. Do this until you have a short list of points that you think have been transmitted via body language.

'Silent' Television

Use your video recorder to tape a 10-minute segment of your favourite television drama. Then, when you have a few quiet moments to yourself, replay the video recording with the sound off so that you have only the images to go by. Take notes of what the characters seem to be expressing to each other, using the skills listed above.

Once you have completed this exercise, replay the video, but this time with the sound on. Compare your notes from the silent viewing with what the characters are actually saying to each other. How accurate was your interpretation of their body language?

Street Life

Daily routines are usually so hectic that there is often little time to sit and watch the world go by. But so much can learned from doing just that. Occupy the window seat in a cafe or restaurant situated on a busy street. Then simply watch the people passing by, whether they are alone, in couples, or in groups. Make an effort to read their body language. Try to assess the quality and type of relationships you perceive, and what people might be communicating to each other. Unfortunately you can't check out the accuracy of your perceptions on this one – but you'll find that this exercise is good fun!

In the Park

Family life is best observed in a recreational or leisure setting because that's the time when everyone is most relaxed (hopefully) and when they have time to be with each other. Go to the park with your child and sit down on a bench while she plays. Look around at the different families who are also there. Watch how close the adults are to each other, how much physical contact there is between children and their parents, and the type of body language being used. Think about the way this compares with your own family life.

At Home

When your child has a friend over to the house to play – or when she is playing with her brother or sister – sit down unobtrusively in the same room, preferably in a corner where your presence won't be noticed immediately. Try to shut your ears to what they are actually saying (a personal stereo is handy for this). Watch the children at play for a few minutes. The younger your child is, then the more obvious her body language will be. Look at the way the children interact, and pay particular attention to their non-verbal communication.

Knowledge of Body Language

Believe it or not, psychologists have identified almost one million different non-verbal signals! Although this means the science of body language is very complex and detailed, and that there is a lot to learn (this is explained in more detail in subsequent chapters), there are some very basic aspects of your child's body language that you should be able to spot right away when carrying out any 'tuning in' exercises as described above.

Here are some of the more obvious things to look for, just to start with:

eye-contact. When your child is anxious, or when she feels guilty about something, then she won't be able to look you in the eye; instead she will look everywhere except directly at you. Yet when she tells you something she is happy about, her gaze won't stray from yours at all.

breathing. Breathing conveys a great deal of information about your child's feelings. For instance, if you watch closely you'll notice a difference in her rate of breathing when she is angry and upset (short breaths, spaced closely together) and when she is fast asleep (long breaths, spaced further apart).

social distance. The gap left between your child and you during normal conversation is usually between 45 and 60 cm (18 and 24 inches); greater than this might indicate that she is in a bad mood with you (such as when she walks away so that she's not in the same room as you), while less could be a sign that she is angry (such as when she pushes her face furiously into yours).

arm and hand movements. When a child is in a temper, the chances are that she'll clench her fists tightly together, and may press them to the sides of her head. When she feels relaxed and happy, her hands and arms will probably dangle freely by her sides. Rapid hand and arm movements suggest she is frightened by something.

posture. If your child stands in a hunched posture with her shoulders sagging, her head tilting down, then she probably feels miserable or even ashamed. However, the opposite message is conveyed when she stands upright with her shoulders held firmly back and her head positioned so that she's looking straight ahead.

facial expressions. Most facial expressions have an obvious meaning – for instance, a frown indicates fear, worry or confusion, a smile indicates happiness, sparkling eyes tell you that your child feels self-confident, and a trembling lower lip is a sign of impending tears. A grimace is her way of saying she disapproves or that she is in pain.

mobility. Once your child is able to walk independently, she can use her body movements expressively. For instance, you know what she is telling you if she turns her back during the middle of a conversation, or runs to the door and kicks it fiercely! Likewise, snuggling up close to you tells you that she feels comfortable being with you.

Other Factors

Actually interpreting your child's body language on a specific occasion will also depend on other factors, and it is important that you are aware of them. For instance, **the context in which your child uses non-verbal communication** affects the message that she conveys.

Take something as simple as laughter. When a 5-year-old child chuckles loudly you would normally interpret this as a sign of a healthy sense of humour. However, suppose you saw that she laughed in response to something unpleasant, such as her older brother tripping and falling – then you would probably interpret the laughter as a sign of her feelings of antagonism towards her brother. Or suppose you realized she laughed when every other child around her was crying – you would probably suspect there was more to her laughter than simply an expression of her sense of humour.

Therefore, the context of non-verbal communication matters, and affects its significance. Your interpretation should consider the context in which the body language occurs. Use that information to help you to understand the message your child conveys.

Each dimension of body language can take on a different meaning **when it occurs as part of a cluster.** The facial expression of frowning, for instance, could mean that your child is telling you 'Help me. I don't like this.' Yet, if that same facial expression is also accompanied by signs of nervousness – such as clasping her hands tightly together, blinking rapidly and swallowing frequently – then her non-verbal message might be 'Help me, I'm afraid.' This is far removed from the meaning of the frown on its own. Alternatively, your child's frown might also be accompanied by the gestures of scratching her head and then gently stroking her chin; in that case, her body language is probably telling you 'Help me. I'm puzzled and I'm not sure what to do here.'

When practising your skills at interpreting your child's body language, you will be tempted to focus on one gesture at a time, because that's the easiest way. But this will inevitably limit the accuracy of your understanding. Instead, pause for a moment or two before interpreting, reflecting on any other aspects of body language that are operating at the same time, then interpret the entire cluster of gestures together.

Your **background knowledge of your own child** also reveals a lot to you, because you will have a clearer idea of the meaning of specific gestures. For instance, you will know how she stands when she is excited, the tone of voice she uses and her typical facial expression. You have seen that distinctive pattern many times and have no difficulty understanding what it means.

Whenever the knowledge you have of your child's body language runs counter to the typical sorts of body language associated with children her age, follow what you know. In other words, accept your child's individuality in terms of the way she expresses herself nonverbally. Don't worry too much that other children express themselves in different ways. Use your prior experiences with your child to make an accurate interpretation of how she is feeling and what she is trying to tell you.

It's worth bearing in mind that **there are cultural differences** in the expressions and interpretation of body language. Psychological investigations have revealed that, in Britain, a raised brow suggests puzzlement and confusion, whereas in Thailand the same facial expression means unhappiness; facial expressions in Japan are rarely used to convey negative emotions; a ring made by the thumb and forefinger is a sign used in Britain to give the message that everything is all right, whereas in France that gesture means the exact opposite; people from the Middle East tend to look at each other more during a conversation than do people from Britain or North America; parents in America touch their children more frequently than Japanese parents do.

Even basic greetings vary from country to country. British people tend to shake hands with each other when they meet, or even just nod to one another informally; Latin Americans prefer to embrace and pat each other on the back at the same time; in China the preferred mode of greeting is a stiff bow, and this applies to other eastern countries too; Indians greet using their two hands pressed flat together, fingers pointing upwards, with their heads slightly bowed. The next time you travel abroad, see if you can spot any other examples of nonverbal communication that differs from your own.

Faking Body Language to Conceal

You might be worried that your child may be able to 'fake' her body language in order to mask her true feelings. While this is theoretically possible – we can all fake our body language, given enough time and practice – it is extremely unlikely. Children in particular have much more open and direct body language than adults, and this makes it even harder for them to distort their nonverbal communication artificially.

The difficulty facing anybody who tries to fake body language is that faking will only work if it is complete. In other words, every part of the body language has to be consistently false for the pretend message to be received. For example, 6-year-old Donna is upset at not being invited to her friend's party, yet she doesn't want her parents to know that she is distressed. For Donna to conceal her true feelings using body language, not only has she to smile and hide her tears, but she also has to make sure she maintains good eye-contact with her parents when she mentions the incident to them, she has to keep a steady light tone in her voice, she has to make sure her shoulders don't sag or that she doesn't fidget with her fingers, and she has to maintain this performance consistently for the whole day. The chances are that Donna can't keep this facade going for even a few minutes, let alone for several hours. Perceptive parents would quickly see through this faked non-verbal message.

However, there may be times when you have a feeling that your child is giving you mixed messages, times when you feel there is something wrong even though she claims the opposite. Always remember that body language leaks out, and be prepared to inquire a bit further if you are concerned that she is not showing you her genuine feelings.

Using Body Language Positively

Although parents don't want their child to fake body language to conceal emotion, body language can be deliberately manipulated for positive reasons. There may be occasions when your child can purposefully control her non-verbal communication in order to strengthen her relationships with others and to improve the quality of her experiences.

As you will read later in this book, for instance, there

are several body gestures that convey the message of friendliness and openness. Think about your own behaviour when you meet people whom you know and like. You will smile at them, move reasonably close to them (probably 45–60 cm away from them), make regular and long eye-contact, nod approvingly when they relate their latest news to you, and breathe calmly and regularly. Your hands will be open and your posture relaxed. These silent signals tell your friends that you are pleased to see them, and this backs up your verbal communications when you speak to them. You can teach these socially-positive gestures to your child at home – increasing her social skills, perhaps with the knock-on effect of increasing her popularity.

Similarly with non-verbal signals that convey the attitude of caring and sensitivity. Watch someone who acts in a caring way towards another person in distress. There will be a closeness between them, and the carer will have a sympathetic expression, will talk in a quiet tone, will make caring gestures such as placing a hand gently on the other person's arm, and will nod reassuringly as the other person speaks. Again, these components of body language, and their significance, can be taught to your child in order to enhance her relationships with others.

The positive and deliberate use of body language in this way is not devious, however. Unlike faking, which is designed to hide one's true feelings, the considered use of body language is designed to heighten others' awareness of our true feelings. It strengthens the message being conveyed by spoken language. (In

Chapter 7, you will discover how to use this technique to encourage your child's social and emotional development.)

Action Plan for Understanding Your Child's Body Language

The action plan below offers guidance on how to understand your child's body language effectively, and encapsulates many of the points raised earlier – the action plan doesn't guarantee accurate interpretations every time, but it can provide you with a starting point:

Keep it fun. If you take it all too seriously, then you can create problems for yourself. Of course the relationship between you and your child will be strengthened as your ability to understand her body language improves – but it is strong anyway. Interpreting her body language should be more fun than serious.

If possible, spend time every couple of days just watching your child in her normal routine. It's quicker to listen to her spoken language than her nonverbal language, but all you need to do is take a couple of minutes each day to observe her facial expressions and her body movements.

Look for clusters, as well as solitary gestures. A gesture your child uses, such as tapping herself on the head, can mean anything from confusion to boredom. Yet this same gesture can indicate something different depending on the rest of her body language. So look at what else she is doing at the same time; this increases the accuracy of your interpretations.

Interpret her body language in different circumstances. You will probably discover that she uses different body language gestures with, say, her close friends, than she does with you. The more you watch her, the more you will see the full range of her body language.

Try to verify your interpretation. You may, for instance, deduce that your child's non-verbal communication is telling you she is afraid or uncertain. Once you have reached that conclusion, ask her if in fact she does feel this way – this enables you to confirm whether or not your interpretation is correct.

Remember that everybody uses body language. Adults and children transmit and receive non-verbal communications all the time – and they haven't had any special training in these skills. So the likelihood is that you are probably better at interpreting body language than you think.

Watch her when she's involved in pretend play. A young child uses role-play or dressing-up games to express her feelings, as well as to enjoy herself, and this can be another source of non-verbal communication. For instance, pretending to be a bossy adult could be her way of telling you non-verbally that she thinks you are too domineering.

Try using your child's gestures yourself. This is a good way to develop your understanding of her non-verbal communication. Suppose, for instance, that you see her scratching her cheek and tapping her foot quickly, but that you don't know what this means. Copy these actions and consider how you feel as you do so.

If in doubt, ask others what they think your child's body language means. Observing other children objectively is easier than observing your own. You might find it worthwhile to ask for someone else's interpretation of your child's body language, to back up your own ideas.

Make yourself aware of your own body language. Your child is likely to imitate your behaviour, and your non-verbal gestures – so don't be surprised when she puts on a facial expression that you recognize as being one of yours. And if you use that expression when, for instance, you are excited, then she will use it to express excitement as well.

Summary

There is no mystery to the technique of understanding your child's body language. The key skills include having a basic knowledge of the main dimensions of non-verbal communication, the ability to observe, and flexibility in interpretation. Practise using these skills when watching television, or when looking at people passing you in the street. Components of body language include facial expression, posture, social distance, breathing and movement.

The context in which non-verbal communication

occurs affects its meaning; when looking at your child's body language it is better to observe clusters of gestures, rather than individual ones, since the meaning of a particular gesture can change when it is displayed alongside others. Body language is often used differently in different cultures. A child is unlikely to fake her body language, but she can be encouraged to use nonverbal communication deliberately in a positive way to strengthen her social relationships with other children.

Part Two

Body Language in Infancy (0–2 Years)

Chapter Two

What Your Baby Says to You

Born to Communicate

All babies have an inborn need to communicate and interact with those around them. It's as though they arrive in this world already pre-programmed to do this. Proof of this comes from research which shows that babies are born with an amazing set of sensory and perceptual skills, enabling them to begin to communicate with other people:

– **vision.** Within hours of birth, a baby can distinguish his mother's face from that of a stranger; and another study revealed that when babies as young as 9 minutes old are shown a picture of a normal face and a picture of a mixed-up face (the eyes where the nose should be, etc.), they look more closely at the normal face, indicating their preference for it. Newborns can also distinguish the colours red, green, yellow and blue, and can see the difference between drawings of a triangle, cross, circle and square.

– **grasping.** Place your finger in the palm of your newborn baby's hand and you'll find that his fingers encircle it in a grasp which is so tight that you may be able to pull him to a sitting or standing position.

– **reaching.** A newborn reaches out purposefully for objects placed in front of him, although his hand might be closed by the time it makes contact with the object. In a recent study, young babies wearing special goggles which presented the illusion of a reachable object reached for the illusory object and then cried when they discovered they couldn't grab hold of it.

– **touch and balance.** Soon after birth, a baby reacts differently to the touch of brush bristles of different diameters. He will also respond to puffs of air so subtle that even an adult would have difficulty detecting. Although he doesn't have a well-developed sense of balance, he will become sick if spun round too suddenly and he'll try to right his head if placed in an awkward position.

– **taste and smell.** New babies make distinct facial expressions when they experience sweet, sour and bitter tastes, expressions which match those of adults experiencing the same tastes. A sense of smell is also present soon after birth; a baby will make a positive facial expression when smelling a fruit odour, and an expression of disgust when smelling fishy odours. Research has also shown that a newborn will turn towards the smell of a breast pad his mother has worn, but not towards the smell of a breast pad worn by someone else.

– **hearing.** A newborn baby cries at the sound of another baby's cries, but stops when he hears a tape recording of his own cries. This suggests that babies can tell one cry from another. He also prefers the sound of a human voice to any other type of sound he hears, and has a particular preference for his mother's voice. A newborn baby can also discriminate between the noise of a buzzer and the noise of a rattle.

Body Language Is the Only Way

With all these elementary inborn skills, your young baby is ready to start immediately on the process of communicating with you. However, this communication has to be non-verbal simply because he can't speak. He can cry, he can whine, he can laugh, he can giggle, he can wave his arms and legs about (though not in a very controlled and precise way), he can wriggle all over the place, he can make a wide range of facial expressions, he can stare, he can grip, he can turn away – in fact, he can communicate with you in lots of different ways with his body. But he can't speak. So your ability to understand your baby's body language is absolutely crucial if you are to communicate effectively with each other.

Crying

Virtually all parents agree that crying is their baby's most immediate and effective way of communicating. That's hardly surprising, given that babies spend a substantial part of their time engaged in this activity (at least 2 hours each day)! Crying is most frequent in the first three months of life, and then it begins to diminish in frequency so that, by the time he is a year old, he cries for less than an hour a day.

Your baby, like most, will probably scream the place down during the early evening hours, just when you and your family are trying to settle down and relax after a hard day. A surprisingly high number of babies cry constantly, even though there is no obvious reason for their tears. If your baby falls into this group, you can take some reassurance from the fact that he is not the only one. Fortunately, he will grow out of it eventually, and other more sophisticated forms of non-verbal communication take over as your baby develops. In the meantime, however, it helps if you can understand what his cries mean.

Understanding Your Baby's Cries

Your baby's cries have different meanings, each type of cry communicating a distinct message to you. As you get to know your baby, you'll tune in to his cries and learn to react in a way that calms him. Remember that he never cries 'just for the sake of it' – there is always a reason. Crying is always due to discomfort, either physical or emotional. Examples of normal crying include:

The 'I want to be fed' Cry. Your baby starts to cry when hungry. This cry that tells you he wants food follows a repetitive sequence, in which he cries, pauses for a moment to catch his breath, cries, pauses for a moment to catch his breath, and so on.

Solution: Give him food until he is no longer hungry.

The 'My nappy is dirty' Cry. Your young baby prefers his nappy to be clean and dry. The cry that stems from the discomfort of a dirty nappy starts off quietly and then gets louder and louder. You'll also notice that he wriggles about in his cot.

Solution: Check his nappy straight away – he probably needs a fresh one.

The 'Something is hurting me' Cry. Every baby cries when he is in pain. This type of cry will be sharp, almost like a shriek, then he'll gasp as he draws in breath, and then the shrieking will continue.

Solution: Try to find out what's hurting him.

The 'Amuse me because I'm fed up' Cry. Babies need stimulation, and boredom sets in if he doesn't get it. This type of cry is designed to get your attention, so it is more like a shout than a cry – and he'll keep shouting like this as long as he feels bored.

Solution: Play with him, sing a song to him, or read a story to him.

The 'Rock me to sleep' Cry. Your baby will become fractious when he is tired, even though he may fight sleep. He'll whine irritably, perhaps nodding off for a couple of seconds, and you may notice that he rubs his hands deep into his eyes and face.

Solution: Gently rock him until he eventually nods off to sleep.

The 'Keep me company' Cry. Your baby is sociable – he likes to have you beside him at all times. When he's feeling lonely and sorry for himself, his cry will be pitiful rather than loud, as though he is sad rather than angry.

Solution: Spend time with him at least until he settles. If you need to get things done, a good solution is to strap him to you in a baby sling and carry on with hanging the clothes out, making yourself something to eat, etc.

The 'There's something wrong with me' Cry. Crying is the only way your baby has of telling you he doesn't feel well, so you have to consider this possibility. A cry due to ill-health can be quite piercing and may be accompanied by lethargic body movements.

Solution: Check there is nothing obvious wrong; call the doctor if you're not sure.

Why Do Babies Cry So Much?

To be honest, scientists don't know why babies use crying so much to communicate their needs, rather than, say, smiling or other non-verbal body movements. However, crying is more effective than these other forms of body language, because:

- It works over long distances. Whereas you can't see him smile at you when you are in another room, you can hear his cry – and he will keep crying until he knows that you have heard him.
- It is a universal sign of distress. You know from your own experience that crying indicates there is something wrong, and therefore you are more likely to respond to a cry than to any other form of communication.
- It is easy for a young baby. He can cry without any effort at all (for instance, even when he is ill and exhausted), whereas smiling or reaching out requires more thought and control; crying is the easy option for him.
- It is a precursor to speech. In a year or so, he'll use his vocal chords to produce speech rather than cries, and he'll be able to communicate his needs more effectively that way. In the meantime, crying exercises his vocalization, which he'll eventually use for speech.

It's as though your baby instinctively knows that crying is his best means of communication, and that he'll be better able to attract your attention that way. True, he does use other aspects of body language in the first year, but crying is always his preferred option.

Ages and Stages:
Patterns of Crying in the First Year

Age

One week   *Description*

You'll find that he cries with almost monotonous regularity, but you will soon learn that his cries most often indicate his desire to progress to the next stage of the day's events (feeding time, cuddle time, nap time, etc.)

Explanation

The main reasons for crying at this age have been listed earlier – they are generally always to do with some form of discomfort (hunger, thirst, tiredness, a nappy that needs to be changed, illness, etc.).

3 months   *Description*

At this age, you may find his cries are very upsetting, especially if he has crying sessions in the early evening. Many babies at this age draw their knees tightly to their tummy when crying.

Explanation

When you seek advice from your health visitor

or doctor about how to soothe your baby, you may be told that he has colic (a very painful type of gastrointestinal disorder). Yet some people (doctors and psychologists among them) believe there is no such condition as colic.

6 months   *Description*
             There will be times when he is perfectly happy, yet suddenly he bursts into tears unexpectedly and for no apparent reason. This often happens when others are present.
             Explanation
             By now, he understands the difference between a familiar face and a face he doesn't recognize – and he is shy in the company of strangers. Don't worry about these tears; they will pass in the next few months as his self-confidence grows.

9 months   *Description*
             Infants at this age have a short fuse, and are ready to erupt in temper at a moment's notice. He may cry from rage at not being able to achieve what he wants.
             Explanation
             He is aware that other children can move about more freely and he wants to be like them. So when there is a toy that isn't within his immediate reach, then his temper erupts and tears of frustration start to flow.

12 months   *Description*
             Don't be surprised to see him crying furiously
             when you take him to parent-and-toddler group
             or when he is with others his own age at home.
             Explanation
             He likes being in the company of other children
             his age, yet still lacks confidence. When another
             child approaches him he becomes afraid and
             tearful. He will cling to you as the tears start
             to fall.

Other Non-Speech Sounds

Your baby uses sounds very purposefully during the
first year, before he has the ability to form words. Like
crying, this early use of sounds is a vital part of his non-
verbal communication skills. Here are some of the
sound-communication stages your baby will go through,
each one approximating speech more closely than the
previous stage, but not resulting in actual words until
around the age of one year at the earliest:

- **cooing.** From between 2 and 5 months, your baby
starts to make regular sounds that at times make you
think he is trying to speak to you. However, unlike
speech, cooing does not communicate meaning but is
often used to attract your attention.
- **babbling (random).** His ability to control the
sounds he makes has matured, largely due to physical
and neurological maturation. Now, his sounds can be
high or low, noisy or loud, sharp or soft – enabling

him to produce a wide range of vocalizations. This babbling of the typical 6-month-old infant is purely random, although you may notice that he tends to use the same strings of sounds consistently. It doesn't take much to start him off – a smile from you or a loving cuddle will be enough to send him into full flow.

– **babbling (controlled).** Your baby gains more command and structure over his babbling in the latter half of the first year. At times you may be convinced he is saying something specific to you, if only you could understand – this is the first genuine sign of early speech. He'll probably play at babbling occasionally, and sit endlessly repeating the same sounds over and over again.

– **early speech.** By 12 months you may have heard his first word. Remember that it doesn't need to sound exactly like the words you use; his first word is simply a recognizable sound sequence that he uses consistently in the same situation to identify the same person or object.

Throughout the period from birth to 12 months, your baby passes specific sound-communication milestones, at approximately the following ages. At 1 month he will turn his head towards you when you speak to him, or turn towards the radio or television when it is switched on. At this stage you will be familiar with his cries, able to tell reliably what each sound means. By the age of 3 months he is more attentive to sounds in his environment; he may stop what he is doing in order to listen keenly. Recognizable sounds such 'wi', 'ba' and 'doh' are common.

A child aged 6 months becomes very interested in pre-verbal communication, trying to engage you in some form of verbal interaction even though he can't talk yet. Sometimes he will stop babbling in order to let you say something, as if he is having a normal conversation with you. He makes a range of distinctive babbling sounds. And by 9–12 months, his babbles combine to form different clusters, which he starts to use consistently and reliably. For instance, he might use 'nata' whenever he sees the dog, or 'baba' whenever he sees his brother. These words make sense to him, if not, at first, to you.

Talking to Your Baby Boosts Non-verbal Communication

Perhaps you feel silly talking to your young baby – because he can't respond verbally or because you know you have to rely on body language. Yet talking to your young baby stimulates his later language development – and his non-verbal communication skills – for a number of reasons, including:

It encourages him to use his communication skills. Although your baby has no real understanding of what you say to him, he does recognize that you are connecting with him. And he enjoys this connection, this interaction, despite his developmental limitations at this stage. As a result, he tries harder to communicate non-verbally with you.

It provides a model for him to copy. He watches your face closely when you speak to him, and notices non-verbal dimensions such as your expression (tense or relaxed), your mouth position (open and smiling or closed and tight), and your eyes (sparkling or dull). He will begin to copy some of these aspects in time.

It reduces his frustrations. The more relaxed your baby is, then the more likely he is to communicate with you in any way that he can (that is, through body language). Talking to him, telling him stories and singing him songs all help him to feel relaxed and comfortable, and put him in a more communicative mood.

So don't feel silly or embarrassed talking to your baby. It helps strengthen the emotional attachment between you, while gently stimulating his communication skills (both verbal and non-verbal). It also makes life more interesting for both of you!

Smiling, Grimacing and Other Common Baby Facial Expressions

The other main channel of body language used by your baby is facial expressions – these convey so much information to you, especially once you get to know his individual expressions.

Compared to those of older children and adults, babies' facial expressions differ in two significant ways. First, an infant has a narrower range of facial expressions in the first year of life than he does in later childhood. This makes it easier for you to interpret the meaning of the look on your baby's face, because there is less variety. Second, a baby is less likely to make a particular facial expression deliberately in order to achieve a particular response – his facial expression is entirely spontaneous. As he grows older, he will learn that certain looks (such as a frown or a scowl) nearly always elicit a negative response from other people, whereas others (such as a smile) will nearly always be greeted with a positive response. But your baby is totally unaware of this during the first year. That's why his facial expressions are more genuine, more spontaneous, without any underlying purpose other than to reveal his true feelings, and there are plenty of emotions your baby can convey to you using just the few expressions at his disposal. The chart below lists them.

Emotion	Facial Expression
Happiness and pleasure	Broad smile, eyes sparkling. When you see this you will have no doubt what it means! The first smile usually appears around the age of 6 weeks, and remains a fixed part of your child's non-verbal communication from then on. Smiling in this context is frequently accompanied by animated

	hand and legs movements, vigorous enough to shift his cot blanket, for example.
Satisfaction and contentment	Small smile, relaxed facial muscles. You will probably see this on his face just after a feed, and it is a sign that he feels contented. Unlike the broad smile with its vigorous body movements, this smile is accompanied by calmness and a general lack of arm and leg movements. Your baby's hunger has been satisfied – and this shows in his face.
Disgust and distaste	Face screwed up, as though he has just tasted something sour. Research shows that babies use the same type of look on their faces as adults do when they want to express distaste – the muscles around the mouth and eyes tense up. You will see this when he tastes something he doesn't like, or even smells something he doesn't like.
Unhappiness, discomfort and pain	Similar to the expression of disgust, but accompanied by piercing cries. Within a few days – or even hours – you will learn to recognize the pattern of non-verbal communication that signifies your baby is unhappy. Try to establish the source of his distress, and then take the necessary action to restore his sense of well-being.

Shock and surprise	Eyes wide open, mouth partially open, with very tense facial muscles. Every baby is born with the startle (Moro) reflex, which is seen either when he is moved suddenly or when he hears a sudden loud noise. As well as opening his hands, arching his back and then bringing his arms together, he will have an unmistakable look of shock on his face.
Fear	Eyes wide open, mouth closed but tense. Research suggests that a baby begins to feel fear from the age of 3 months on. Sudden changes in the environment may cause your baby to be afraid, for instance putting his bedroom light out, or leaving his line of vision quickly. When he does feel fear, it will show on his face.
Anger	Eyes open but tightly screwed up, mouth slightly open, lips slightly parted and very tensed. Your baby can become angry over many things, such as not being fed on time, not getting enough attention, or feeling too restrained. The look of anger on his face will also be accompanied by an irregular cry.
Sadness	Mouth closed, eyes open, brow slightly furrowed. Some babies have this type of expression just before they

fall asleep, but if your baby looks like this and doesn't appear to be tired, then he may simply be feeling miserable. The chances are that all he needs is to be picked up, cuddled and played with for a while.

Arm and Leg Movements

Your baby's physical movements develop gradually during the first year. In the beginning he appears to wriggle about uncontrollably and unpredictably, but some order and structure eventually appear. Put him on his back in his cot when he is about 3 months old; you will see that he kicks his arms and legs in a more synchronized manner. At 6 months, he can push his shoulders off the floor when placed face-down on the carpet, or he can roll from side to side if he decides that is what he wants to do; his legs are stronger too. The typical infant aged 9 months can crawl along the floor in a more coordinated way, drawing his knees under his tummy in his attempts to move forward. He may also be able to support his own weight when you hold his hands, so that he can stand upright. And by one year, he is confident at crawling, sometimes tries to climb up and down stairs (though might become anxious during his attempts), and probably tries to walk round the room holding on to the furniture for support.

This increasing ability to coordinate his arm and leg movements means that your baby is increasingly able to use these to communicate non-verbally. Here are some messages that he might communicate with you using body movements:

'I'm having a thoroughly good time.' His legs, arms and hands will move about very actively, perhaps at a rate that initially makes you concerned. But he is simply expressing his pleasure and excitement. You'll also notice that he has a contented expression on his face and might be making gentle sounds, too.

'I don't feel good.' He'll be restless and will wriggle about. The feeling of pain or discomfort could be strong enough to encourage him to shift position in the hope of finding relief; he may even try pushing himself about. If he is ill, then his face will be in a grimace.

'I want to get that toy.' You suddenly realize that he is face down on the floor, spread out with his arms stretching in front of him. In addition, he stares straight ahead at a particular object, and will also make accompanying gasping sounds which reflect his efforts and frustration.

'I'm not going to eat this.' As you sit before him in his high-chair, looking forward to feeding him his lunch, you find that somehow he manages to hit the spoon away every time it comes near his mouth. He may even be smiling as he does this, although you probably won't find this non-verbal communication very funny.

The Five 'I's – How Your Baby Learns Body Language

Your baby's use of body language increases naturally, as he matures. However, psychological research shows that it is also affected by your own behaviour, especially in the period from birth to 1 year. The main factors to consider include:

1 **Imitation.** Your baby soon begins to imitate your facial expressions, even though you may not realize he is doing this; imitation is a natural part of the bonding process that goes on between parent and baby. That's one of the reasons why you find his facial expressions so easy to understand – they often match yours exactly! Of course, he has his own unique characteristics, but the chances are that many of his non-verbal mannerisms are a reflection of your own.

2 **Intensity.** There are times when your baby doesn't know how to react, and in this situation his reaction will depend almost entirely on your reaction. At the age of 6–9 months, for example, your baby occasionally wakes up from a sleep neither crying nor smiling; he has a neutral, tired expression on his face. If you smile strongly he'll smile in reply; if you display anger, then he'll react with distress. The intensity of your own body language influences your baby's use of body language.

3 **Incidence.** Understandably, the more you use body language to communicate with your baby then the

more he's likely to use it too. Talking to your baby, playing with him and generally providing a high level of stimulation in the first year are all important for his overall development. But these activities also help him to develop early communication skills. So make lots of opportunities for interacting with him, in ways that he can see you clearly. Face-to-face games and songs are particularly helpful.

4   **Interaction.** Psychological research, involving video recordings of mothers and their babies playing together, has revealed that a baby tends to synchronize his babbling and other sounds with his mother's speech. When the video tapes are slowed down, they confirm that when the mother talks, the baby is quiet, and then when she is finished, he starts to babble, as though they are taking part in a 'pre-conversation'. In these pre-speech activities, your baby learns the non-verbal actions that accompany spoken language.

5   **Intonation.** One of the main features of a mother's speech towards her baby is that it is accompanied by an exaggerated speech intonation. When you talk to your baby in this way, you make your intonation more extreme so that high sounds are higher than normal, low sounds are lower than normal, and your speech pattern is generally more vivid than when talking, say, to an older child. This increased variation in intonation engages your baby's attention, encouraging him to focus on your non-verbal communication, too.

Summary

Your baby arrives in this world already pre-programmed to interact with you, and since he can't use language to communicate till the second year at the earliest, he has to rely on body language. If you and your baby can understand each other's non-verbal communication, your relationship strengthens.

With many babies, crying is the main channel of non-verbal communication. Your baby's cries can have many different meanings, but you will soon tune in to these; sometimes, though, you will have no idea at all why he's crying so vigorously. The pattern of crying changes between birth and 12 months, as your baby develops his pre-speech skills. He also begins to use other sounds, such as cooing and babbling to communicate with you. Another dimension of body language at this stage in life is facial expression – your baby can convey a whole series of emotions just by varying the look on his face. Bear in mind that, although his use of non-verbal communication grows spontaneously, the way you relate to him is also very important because your body language influences his.

Chapter Three

What Your Toddler Says to You

Changes

Between the ages of 1 and 2 years your child changes dramatically, and this affects her non-verbal communication with you. For instance, she starts to learn to walk – hence the term 'toddler'. Being more independent, she can voyage into new territory without your help, and her natural curiosity increases as she learns new things every day. Like most parents, you'll probably find that during this period your child becomes very difficult and demanding, especially if she doesn't get her own way – temper tantrums are common at this age. Changes in your child's understanding of herself make her feel self-important, and she doesn't like rules (unless, of course, she makes them!).

This stage of your child's development is also marked by a change in the way she uses body language.

There are several reasons for this:

Spoken language becomes her preferred means of communication. From the age of 12 to 18 months, your toddler starts to develop spoken language and this process continues throughout the preschool years and beyond. Even when she can only say single words, she is able to use these to communicate with you very effectively, whereas before she depended entirely on non-verbal communication. For instance, she lets you know when she doesn't want to do something (as when she says 'no') or when she *does* want something (as when she says 'drink'). Words are her first choice for communication.

Her body movements are more controlled. At this age, your toddler's coordination is still immature but it has developed sufficiently to allow her greater control over her muscles and her arm and leg movements. As a result, her body language becomes more varied and expressive. For instance, she can now bring her hand to scratch the back of her neck (conveying to you that she is puzzled), or cross her legs and lean forward while sitting facing you (conveying to you that she is attentive). Her repertoire of body language, therefore, grows significantly.

Her emotions become more varied and intense. The typical toddler is fascinated by the world around her, and is determined to explore in search of new knowledge and experiences. Her range of emotions also increases and she feels things more intensely. For instance, she now attempts many activities which are too demanding for her (such as opening a box, switching on the television) and this arouses her frustration and anger; she is able to take part in energetic play, on swings and roundabouts, which produces levels of excitement that she has probably not experienced before.

She thinks about non-verbal communication. Her ability to use spoken language does not mean she abandons body language altogether. On the contrary, aside from involuntary non-verbal communication, your toddler's greater maturity means that she can begin to use body language quite deliberately to communicate with you. That's why gestures at this age often appear exaggerated, as when she howls with bitterness if she drops a doll out of reach, then stops crying the moment you picked it up for her. Her body language is very effective because it leaves you in no doubt about what she is trying to express.

Socialization lets her learn about other children's body language. Being a toddler, she becomes more interested in the behaviour of the other children she mixes with. And it doesn't matter whether or not she actually talks to them – she'll study other toddlers closely, apparently fascinated by their actions. Through this, your toddler learns how other children use body language. This affects her own pattern of non-verbal communication. For instance, at parent-and-toddler group she soon learns that a child who smiles is probably friendly and a child who frowns is probably less friendly.

Toddler Emotions

The chart below lists the major emotional dimensions of your child's life between the ages of 1 and 3, and looks at ways these are most commonly expressed. Each of these dimensions affects your toddler's body language.

Toddler Emotion	How It Is Expressed
Curiosity	She explores everywhere. Nothing is taboo for her, unless told otherwise, and she is determined to explore every cupboard, every ornament and every single object she can reach and touch.
Challenge	For the first time, she begins to challenge your authority. She is far more concerned about what she wants than about what you want – and she prefers to push against the limits you set for her.
Frustration	When things don't go her way, her frustration can build up quickly. Patience is at a premium at this age, and tantrums are very common – one minute she's calmly playing, the next minute she explodes with rage.
Independence	Your toddler wants to do things for herself (whether or not she is capable of them), and she may become very upset if she can't achieve a particular

	target of independence, such as pulling her socks off.
Shyness	She likes new experiences but may be shy when she sees people she doesn't know well. In these circumstances she may cling to you tightly, afraid to let go of your hand.
Pleasure	Your toddler enjoys life to the full, taking great delight out of the new experiences each day brings. The company of other children, and inter-action with them, becomes more important to her.

Recognizing Your Toddler's Emotions Through Her Body Language

Curiosity

Experimentation is the order of the day, as your child tries out new ways of playing with objects. At 12 months, for instance, she may slowly push her spoon off the high-chair, then hit it quickly away, then gently drop it off the side, and so on, each time finding new ways of making the spoon hit the ground. She's not being naughty – just naturally curious.

By the time your toddler is 2 she begins to develop the ability to use symbolism, which means she can now use one object to represent another. A building brick can 'be-come' an elephant, and a doll can 'become' her big sister.

And her ability to totter about on her own two feet allows her to explore places that she could not reach before.

Here are five ways your toddler uses body language to tell you 'I don't understand what's going on and I want to know more':

1 **frowning facial expression.** With a child of this age, a frown often indicates that she is confused and doesn't fully grasp the meaning of events – it need not indicate that she is angry. Her eye muscles will be tense, a few small lines will appear just above her eyebrows, and her lips may pucker slightly.

2 **leans forward and stares.** Although this may appear rude – if an adult behaved in this way you would certainly think so – it's a sign of her inquisitiveness. Instead of telling her that it's not nice to stare (because as far as she is concerned, it's wonderful to stare), try to establish what she is uncertain about.

3 **moves very close.** A toddler at this stage is frequently unaware of social distance; she may completely fail to appreciate that other people are uncomfortable with someone standing right beside them, looking at them square in the eye. But that's precisely what your child will do if she is curious about someone she sees.

4 **pokes and touches.** Through touch and handling, your child learns about the world around her, about the qualities and characteristics of objects in her environment. This is a natural expression of her curiosity, even though this type of behaviour makes you anxious (for example, in case she drops a valuable ornament she is investigating in this way).

5 **pulls you in a specific direction.** When she sees something or someone that she is unsure of, her first reaction may be to pull you over towards it, in the hope that you will be able to offer her an explanation. Without saying anything, she assumes you will know her underlying intentions.

Tips for Responding to Your Toddler's Curiosity

The most important help you can give is to ensure that you don't misread your child's signs of curiosity as signs of 'naughtiness'. She isn't old enough to consider the consequences of her explorations, and therefore her actions are aimed at discovering new things, not at causing havoc. Provide her with lots of opportunities to develop her curiosity. Of course, she can explore and discover without your help, but her desire to learn will increase if her surroundings are stimulating.

Your toddler will decide how far she is prepared to venture and she won't go further than her self-confidence allows. When her non-verbal communication tells you that she wants to learn more, however, you can encourage her appropriately, perhaps by reassuring her that she has no need to be afraid, or by giving her permission to explore that bit further. Yet be prepared to set limits on your child's curiosity if you have to. Explain that certain items (or certain areas of the house) are out of bounds, and redirect her curiosity elsewhere.

Challenge

Toddlers are so full of their own importance. All that matters is what they want. So when your toddler decides that she wants a biscuit *now*, she has to have it now whether or not you hold the same opinion. And she will simply ignore what you say if it doesn't tie in with her immediate wishes. Rules that mum and dad set are there to be broken, as far as she's concerned, as are rules set by other children. The only person allowed to set rules is your child! She challenges your authority because she wants to be the one who makes all the decisions.

Here are five ways your toddler uses body language to tell you 'I know this is what you want me to do, but I intend to do what I want':

1 **blank facial expression.** When you give her an instruction, or set a limit on her behaviour, instead of responding she may take on a completely blank and neutral expression, as though she hasn't heard what you have said – she has, it's just that she wishes she hadn't.

2 **pushes past you.** Even though you are not physically blocking her desired goal, she may try to push past you, as though this is the same as pushing past your rules. In your toddler's mind, you and your limits are one and the same – so if she can get round one, she can get round the other.

3 **folds her arms.** Folding arms in front of the body is one of the most primitive ways of showing both strength and annoyance. She doesn't like what you

have said to her, and wrapping her arms round herself, or folding them, is her non-verbal way of telling you that she doesn't accept what you say – she wants to challenge you.

4 **continues even though you have told her to stop.** Even though she hasn't said a word in defiance of your authority, this is the one action that is most likely to anger you because it is a clear rejection of your wishes. Her behaviour indicates that she has no intention of listening to what you have said to her.

5 **stomps up to you, stares you closely in the face.** When your toddler marches angrily towards you, moving her face to within an inch or two from yours, you will have no doubt that your authority is under attack. This type of gesture is designed to be threatening; she hopes you will back down.

Tips for Responding to Your Toddler's Challenges to Your Authority

Part of growing up involves learning to take other people's points of view into account, and learning to think of the feelings of other people. Your toddler isn't able to do this as yet – hence her determination to do what she wants no matter how you might feel about this at the time.

Don't give in to her, even though her challenges are ongoing. At this stage she require a consistent and structured discipline that provides her with a sense of security; inconsistent discipline at home – or lack of discipline – confuses and frightens a young child. Discipline also encourages her to become sensitive to the needs and wants of others, and leads to self-control. In the meantime, she needs you to be firm and to stand your ground. So do just that.

Frustration

At the toddler stage, your child has little ability to tolerate frustration – the feeling that arises when she does not succeed at an activity. Her temper rises very quickly when her goal is not achieved – and you don't need to be an expert in reading body language to know when she's having a tantrum! Anything can trigger her frustration (such as your refusal to allow her to play with a particular toy, her inability to place a piece of a puzzle in the correct place, the news that she has to go to bed now). In time her threshold of frustration will increase, but in these early years it does not take much to make her feel frustrated and irritable – she has a short fuse, leading to a quick temper.

Here are five ways your toddler uses body language to tell you 'I'm feeling frustrated because I can't do what I want, and I'm getting ready to explode':

1 **laboured breathing.** One of the first signs of frustration build-up is that your child's breathing becomes more noticeable to you. It changes from its normal pattern to shallow and rapid, and louder than usual. Your child may start to breathe heavily through her nose, instead of her mouth. A tantrum is not far way.

2 **clenched fists.** As the tension inside her builds up, her muscles tense too – this is an outward indication of inner stress. Being a toddler, she will make little attempt to hide this feeling, and the easiest place for it to reveal itself is in her hand muscles. Even if you can't see her face, her clenched hand muscles will tell you she is frustrated and angry.

3 **rocking body movements.** Your toddler may find the frustration so difficult to bear that she feels the need to rock back and forth, in a type of comforting motion. This can ease her tense feeling. The rocking motion may be soft and smooth, but if she is very frustrated these movements may be jerky and sharp.

4 **gritted teeth.** Jaw muscles become tight, and teeth become clenched together. This is her involuntary muscular reaction to feelings of frustration. Sometimes the jaw muscles are so tightly constricted that you can actually hear your toddler grinding her upper and lower sets of teeth together.

5 **throws things.** If she is playing with a toy or puzzle that isn't going the way she intends, her non-verbal reaction to frustration may be to pick the object up and cast it away to the other side of the room. She's not being naughty – removal of the object causing frustration may be enough to remove her frustration. This may stop a tantrum occurring.

Tips for Responding to Your Toddler's Frustration

You probably have difficulty coping with frustration, so you should not be surprised when your toddler has difficulty too. Bear in mind that frustration is not the same as temper, though a build up to frustration can lead to a tantrum; therefore it is best to dissipate your toddler's frustration before that point is reached.

When you see by her body language that she is agitated, help her regain control of the situation. Of course, you can simply remove the source of her frustration or remove her from the source; although this is a sensible short-term solution, it doesn't teach her how to cope with these feelings in the long term. A more effective strategy is to encourage her to take action herself. First, acknowledge her frustration. Tell her that you can see she is unhappy and that you don't think she should continue with that activity. Secondly, suggest that she leave it for the moment and try again later in the day. Thirdly, encourage her to remain calm.

Independence

The problem with a toddler's desire to do everything herself is that her ambition usually far outstretches her capabilities. For instance, she may want to get herself a biscuit from the tin in the kitchen, but hasn't yet got the necessary skills to reach the tin, or even to open it. However, this doesn't stop her trying. Every day there will be examples of her determination to manage without your help (although there will also be plenty of times when she still depends on you).

Here are five ways your toddler uses body language to tell you 'I'm determined to do this by myself, without your help':

1 **secrecy.** Don't be surprised to find that your toddler has silently gone off somewhere to practise, for instance, putting on a shoe. She's not being devious – this is simply her way of making sure she has some peace and quiet on her own to try this activity for herself. She may feel the need for this type of privacy.

2 **pushes you away.** The only thing she can do when you try to help her with something (assuming she doesn't want your help) is to reject you by pushing your hand away from her. She may not be able to say that she doesn't want your help, but this specific gesture is her non-verbal way of expressing that feeling.

3 **persists at an activity.** A toddler's concentration span is not very long, as she quickly moves from one activity to another. However, the desire to achieve a goal without help often results in her persistence with an activity for longer than would normally be expected. The determination for independence intensifies her concentration.

4 **'set' facial expression.** Her face is likely to have a fixed, possibly even blank, expression, as she struggles to do whatever it is that she wants to. The need to complete the task requires her to focus all her attention, and hence the rather rigid look spread right across her face.

5 **tears.** Remember that she's still only a toddler, and tears come very easily to a child this age; it doesn't take much to trigger the flow. The fact that she wants to manage by herself doesn't mean that she can

realize this ambition every time – crying, stemming from self-pity and self-directed anger, may result from her lack of success.

Tips for Responding to Your Toddler's Need for Independence

Encouraging your child to be independent during the toddler stage can be tiresome and demanding – it's hard work for you and her. Try to be supportive, however. Her independence will only improve in gradual stages, and she will fail in her efforts if she tries to do too much too soon. Encourage her to progress slowly and steadily, rather than in giant leaps. Remember that she needs your reassurance – a word of encouragement, or an approving smile, is all that is required.

She may be impatient to succeed, so slow her down. Suggest that she should take her time, and not rush things. And if she tries to complete an activity independently but does not achieve her goal, praise her for any part of it she has achieved and reassure her that she can always try again. Emphasize to her that she makes progress every time she tries, and that she will get there eventually.

Shyness

The typical toddler is full of confidence – until she sees someone she doesn't know. Then she is overcome by shyness and an overwhelming desire to hide herself. Sometimes this shyness is obvious, but other times she may try to conceal these feelings of embarrassment;

either way she will be uncomfortable when meeting new children and adults for the first time. Of course, she will probably grow out of this eventually, but for the time being shyness is her first reaction to an unfamiliar face.

Here are five ways your toddler uses body language to tell you 'I'm shy and I don't want to talk to any of these people':

1 **holds your hand tightly.** This is a sure sign that she is shy of an unfamiliar child or adult. As far as your toddler is concerned, she is safe and secure as long as she can see you and touch you. And the more tightly she holds your hand when someone approaches, then the safer she feels.

2 **presses her body against your body.** You may find that she leans so heavily into you that she almost unbalances you. Or you may find that she literally hides herself behind you in the presence of someone she doesn't know very well. This is her attempt to make herself 'invisible'.

3 **no eye-contact.** A child who is shy will not feel comfortable looking at a stranger. Instead of the normal eye-contact, your toddler will cast her eyes downwards towards the ground, refusing to look upwards even when you ask her to do so. It's as though she believes that if she doesn't look at the person, then he or she will go away.

4 **covers her eyes.** A toddler doesn't yet have the maturity to realize that other people remain there, whether or not she can actually see them. In her shyness, therefore, she may put her hands across her eyes, obscuring her vision altogether. That solves her

problem temporarily, and may make her feel more confident as a result.

5 **face reddens.** This aspect of non-verbal communication has different meanings, depending on the particular circumstances. However, if your toddler's face goes deeply red when an unfamiliar child or adult approaches, then the chances are that she feels overwhelmed by shyness at that moment.

Tips for Responding to Your Toddler's Shyness

Be patient with your toddler. Her shyness may be irritating for you – and it may even embarrass you in front of other parents – but she can't help it. In fact, she would be delighted if she didn't feel so miserable when meeting a new child. So avoid reprimanding her for being impolite, or trying to jolly her out of it by making fun of her shyness. Reassure her that she will be fine, that she has nothing to worry about. And if she wants to bury her face against you at first, let her.

Shyness often decreases with social experience. In other words, the more your toddler mixes with other children her own age, the better. Take her along to a parent-and-toddler group if there is one in the area, and invite family and friends with young children over to play with her if possible. With your gentle encouragement, she will soon mix with others quite happily, although she may always have an element of shyness. That's perfectly normal.

Pleasure

As long as your child's basic physical and psychological needs are satisfied, then she will feel content with herself and the world around her. However, the typical toddler swings from joy to distress at a moment's notice, often without any sign of warning. And this happens the other way, too: she may scream with unhappiness that she can't watch her favourite television programme, as though her world has come to an end, yet quickly compose herself when the prospect of a biscuit and glass of juice looms on the horizon.

Here are five ways your toddler uses body language to tell you 'I'm happy with what is happening and I'm having great fun':

1 **animated facial expression.** Your toddler will usually show her pleasure in her face. When she is happy about something she will have a broad smile, her eyes will be wide open, and she may even laugh or giggle. Her whole facial expression is lively, excited and sparkling.
2 **very active body movements.** You will notice that she moves her arms and legs more quickly when she is happy. Her general manner is alert, lively and enthusiastic. She may march about the house in a bright and breezy manner, with light footsteps, singing happily to herself as she moves along.
3 **interested in her surroundings.** Like you, she takes a greater interest in events around her when she is happy. She notices things that she appeared to ignore

before. Suddenly, she becomes fascinated by what you are doing at the time and may want to help you with that activity or imitate your actions.

4 **sits close to you.** When your toddler feels happy and contented, she is relaxed. She will probably want to snuggle up close beside you, not because she feels insecure or anything like that, but because she feels satisfied and wants to share this feeling with you. Making body contact with you is one way of doing this.

5 **makes good eye-contact when you talk to her.** When she is happy, her need to challenge you diminishes. She generally becomes more cooperative and responsive, so she is more willing to listen to what you have to say, and to look at you while you are saying it. This strong eye-contact tells you that she's feeling happy.

And here are five ways she uses body language to tell you 'I'm unhappy with what is happening and I'm having a miserable time':

1 **shoulders slumped.** At times when she is unhappy, her muscles will lose their tension and she'll become floppy. Look at her shoulders. Typically they will be held back firmly. But when she is unhappy, you'll see that she becomes round-shouldered as her muscles start to sag.

2 **lethargic.** The youthful enthusiasm of a young toddler can vanish almost immediately in the face of unhappiness. She may lose all interest for her toys, and appear generally lethargic and apathetic, lying

on the floor or on the sofa. When you speak to her, she responds in a sluggish, tired way.

3 **tears.** Crying through unhappiness is different from crying through rage. The latter is accompanied by body tension, clenched fists and very energetic body movements, while the former is altogether less dynamic. The tears will run down her face, and she may say nothing to you despite your questions.

4 **need for cuddles.** Cuddling is a great source of comfort for her. At times of feeling low and unhappy, she'll want to sit on your lap, with your arms wrapped tightly around her. In addition, she'll slump passively against you, resting her tired head on your shoulder. Her body muscles will feel relaxed and floppy.

5 **withdrawn.** One way that your child demonstrates her unhappiness is by becoming withdrawn from those around her. The normally ebullient toddler becomes distant and remote, not answering anyone who tries to speak to her. Don't mistake this for defiance; she doesn't feel like interacting with anyone at the moment, that's all.

Tips for Responding to Your Toddler's Pleasure/Unhappiness

Whether happy or sad, your child will feel better if she can share her emotions with you. Knowing that you are in tune with her feelings will reduce her unhappiness or increase her pleasure – either way, it does her good. So make her aware that you know how she feels, per-haps simply by telling her or by reflecting her mood in your own facial expression and tone of voice.

Try to ascertain the source of her emotion. If she is happy, then discovering the cause of her pleasure gives you a better understanding and will allow you to re-create the experience for her another time; if she is sad, discovering the cause of her misery can help you figure out how to put things right. Empathy towards your toddler brings the two of you closer together, and gives her a sense of security and stability.

Summary

When your child becomes a toddler, she is able to use spoken language to communicate her ideas, needs and feelings. However, her body language remains an important channel of communication. During this period in her life, the major emotional dimensions appear to be curiosity, the need to challenge, frustration and temper tantrums, the desire for independence, shyness, and pleasure/unhappiness. Each of these emotions shows through in her body language, and it remains crucial for you to be able to read these signals correctly in order to respond to her appropriately and help her along in her emotional development.

Part Three

Body Language
in Childhood
(3–6 + Years)

Chapter Four

New Dimensions in Body Language

As He Matures

From the age of 3 years onwards, your child matures significantly. By the time he is 6 years old he is unrecognizable compared to when he was toddler. The changes that occur during this period are widespread, covering all aspects of his development.

One effect of these changes in maturity is that the principal components of your child's body language begin to resemble those used in adult body language. In other words, there is strong similarity between older children and adults in the way they express non-verbal communication. Of course, a gap remains – adult body language is far more sophisticated – but the main features are remarkably similar. Compared to your child's body language when he was a baby or toddler, his body language at this age and stage is more involved, more varied, more detailed and more complex. You will no longer be able to interpret its meaning so easily, and you'll have to work harder to access what he's trying to say to you.

New dimensions of body language come into usage now, and the existing dimensions mushroom in complexity. The main channels of non-verbal communication from this stage onwards include facial expression, body distance, body posture, eye movements, hand and arm gestures, leg movements and touch. In this chapter, each of these is examined in turn. Remember, though, that the examples given don't automatically apply to your child and that dimensions of body language work in conjunction with each other. But these examples will provide you with guidelines, starting points for a better understanding of your child.

Facial Expression

From now on, your growing child uses his facial expression as the main channel for non-verbal communication. Through this, he can convey a multitude of meanings, each of which can be transmitted by a small change in facial muscles. For instance, it doesn't take much to change a smile into a sneer – all that is required is a small muscle twitch at the side of the mouth; and the simple act of raising an eyebrow changes a smile into a quizzical expression. Facial expression, therefore, is very powerful.

There is a vast array of muscles, neural pathways and nerve cells that are required for every facial expression. If you have ever tried to work a puppet on a string, you will have found how difficult it is to control the puppet's four limbs using a string attached to each limb. Imagine if you had to control a puppet that had thousands of limbs and thousands of ways of activating these different limbs – not easy! Yet this is what your child does when he changes the look on his face. Many different muscles are involved in each section of his face, and these all lead back to a part of the brain which contains several thousand nerve cells. And he does this without any formal training. No wonder scientists believe that the ability to use body language is innate.

How many different emotions do you think you can convey with a look on your face? Try this out in front of a mirror; you may be surprised to find how many different feelings you can communicate this way. Research has confirmed that there are usually only between six and eight emotions that your child successfully conveys through facial expression. These include happiness, shock, rage, unhappiness, fear and disgust. However, there are many ways to convey these emotions facially.

Facial expression is divided into five component parts:

1 head position: when talking to you, your child's head can be held in a variety of positions including upright and facing you (cooperation and willingness to listen), tilted slightly to one side or the other (definite interest and desire to hear more), nodding (approval), shaking (disapproval) or tilted forward (hostility, anger)

2 mouth position: your child's mouth can be smiling (happiness, laughter), down-turned (unhappiness, disappointment), puckered (anger, determination), open (amazement, confusion), slightly open (concentration, curiosity), corner upturned (sneering, disgust) or even and closed (concealed anger, disinterest)

3 eye position: your child's eyes can be wide open (surprise, pleasure, terror, mockery), tightly closed (anger, determination, fear), screwed tightly half-shut (anger, disgust), loosely half-shut (sleepy, relaxed, comfortable) open normally (contentment, relaxation) or sparkling and open (excitement, pleasure, happiness)

4 eyebrows and brow: your child's forehead and eyebrows can be tightly screwed up (anger, determination), completely relaxed (pleasure, comfort, satisfaction), raised and with relaxed facial muscles (confusion, doubt, curiosity), raised and with tense facial muscles (fear, anxiety, pain) or raised and with open mouth (terror, surprise).

5 tongue: although the use of the tongue to convey feeling diminishes in later childhood, it is especially popular at this age and is often used deliberately. Your child's tongue can protrude sharply (rudeness, defiance, anger), protrude slightly (concentration, relaxation, contentment) or lick his lips (thirst, anticipation).

Body Distance

Every child needs his own personal space (also known as 'body distance' because it refers to the distance between himself and the nearest person) and becomes uncomfortable when that space is encroached by others. The amount of personal space he needs at any given time, however, depends on the context. For instance, he doesn't mind you being right beside him, holding his hand, but he would reject the same intrusion into his personal space by a total stranger. And he may not even like you being so close if, for example, he is with his friends. There are many factors to consider. Conversely, your child uses body distance to convey feelings and attitudes non-verbally.

Psychologists studying common patterns in body space have identified four main circles of distance:

1   the intimate circle. This is the area lying within a 45-cm (18-inch) radius of your child's body. He only allows people he knows extremely well to enter this circle (such as you, his siblings, good friends and close relatives) because he is very vulnerable in this area of body space; he needs to trust people for them to approach this close. When someone is in his intimate circle, he can hear them, smell them and touch them, but he can't see their facial expression very clearly because they are so close, so he must feel comfortable before permitting access.

2   the personal circle. This is the area lying within a radius of between 45 cm and 1.2 m (18 in and 4 ft) from your child's body. In normal conversation and day-to-day interaction, your child will maintain this distance from other people. Key sensory experiences associated with the intimate circle (that is, smell,

touch) are unavailable in this circle of body space, but he can see the other person more clearly. It's a safe circle, a circle which renders him less vulnerable than the intimate circle.

3 social circle. This is the area lying within a radius of between 1.2 and 3.6 m (4 and 8 ft) from your child's body. He maintains this distance when he is in more formal, less relaxed situations, for instance when he receives a reprimand from you, or when he wants to ask his teacher a question. Children also use this circle when they have to approach a stranger, for example when they purchase something from a shop. This social distance is not used when your child is relaxed.

4 public circle. This is the area that covers a radius of 3.6 m (8 ft) and outwards from your child's body. You'll rarely see him use this at home because it is the section of personal space reserved for when he is showing his talents to a large group of people. More likely, he'll use this circle, for instance, when performing a song at nursery school, giving a minor recital on the musical instrument that he is just learning to play, or when telling his news to the entire infant class.

An analysis of your child's use of personal space or body distance reveals a great deal about his moods and emotions at the time. When he is angry with you, or perhaps determined to complete an activity on his own without your help, he'll keep you out of the intimate circle; he'll allow you into this space only when he feels relaxed and comfortable, or when he feels insecure and wants a reassuring cuddle. Watch him meet other children for the first time (at playgroup or nursery). You'll see that he keeps them in the social circle and only gradually reduces the distance until they are in the personal circle. Keeping you in the public circle when you are both at home together usually means that he's furious with you!

Body Posture

The position and posture of your child's body when he is with you, or talking to you, communicates his emotions very effectively. For instance, if he walks away from you in the middle of a conversation and turns his back to you, then you can be quite sure he doesn't like what you are saying to him.

Here are some common body positions for you to be aware of:

- standing with hands on hips, facing you square on: this usually indicates his determination and anger. It is a confident stance, challenging and ready for action. Parents are often surprised when their child of this age is so direct.
- sitting on a chair, leaning forward: this usually indicates his interest. If relaxed, leaning forward helps him to concentrate and to focus his attention. However, if tense, leaning forward in his seat may be your child's way of pressing home his argument.
- sitting beside you, but turned to the side: this usually indicates his negative feeling towards you.

Your child stops short of leaving the room altogether, but the angled body position is his way of giving you 'the cold shoulder'.

– standing, hands in pockets: this usually indicates that he is feeling relaxed. Hands in pockets is a very non-aggressive, open gesture, and if he faces you directly in this stance, he feels safe, secure and at ease in your presence.

– sitting or standing with his arms folded. If he is leaning forward, then chances are that he's not in a good mood (folded arms can be an aggressive gesture), but if he's leaning back then chances are that he's happy.

Eye Movements

The eyes are the windows to the soul, according to the popular saying. Most students of body language would agree. In fact, this is reflected in everyday speech, in phrases such as 'looking daggers at you', 'if looks could kill', 'he's got a nasty gleam in his eye', 'he's got a mischievous sparkle in his eye', 'a piercing gaze' and so on.

The most influential part of the eye – in terms of conveying emotions – is the pupil. Watch your child when he is excited; you'll notice that his pupils dilate significantly, perhaps up to three or four times their normal size. This happens because he wants to take in more of his surroundings, and dilating the pupils lets more light in (although this is an involuntary reaction, not deliberate). Likewise, when he is angry at you, he screws up his eyes and his pupils shrink, thereby letting less light in. It's as if by doing so he can't see you so clearly.

The amount of eye-contact made during conversation is important. Psychologists have calculated that the average length of an episode of eye-contact during a normal conversation between parent and child is around 2 seconds before either person breaks away, and that you and your child make mutual eye-contact for roughly one-third of any conversation you have. When your child is listening to you, he'll look at you for approximately 75 per cent of the time, and when he is talking to you he'll look at you for less than half the time. If he makes eye-contact with you for less than a quarter of the time during your conversation, then he may feel guilty about something. When he's very nervous or afraid, he may not be able to make any eye-contact with you at all (in other words, he's 'looking shifty').

Hand and Arm Gestures

Aside from the obvious hand gestures (such as the thumbs-up signal, signifying 'everything's OK') and arm gestures (such as the raised hand, palm facing outwards, signifying the need to stop), there are many more subtle gestures that your child uses as part of his non-verbal repertoire.

Common gestures involving the hands and/or arm, popular with children in this age group include:

- hand covering mouth: this is usually accompanied by a stunned facial expression, indicating that your child is shocked or that he just realized he forgot to tell you an important piece of information he had been entrusted with.

– hand scratching the back of his neck: he feels awkward or even embarrassed – suddenly he has this imaginary itch that he must scratch. This same gesture can mean he is confused, puzzled and uncertain about what to do next.

– hand tight to the top of his head, furrowed brow: he is tense, possibly angry, especially if his hand arrives on his head with smacking force! This gesture is often a prelude to his bursting into tears.

– thumb or finger inside his mouth: children of this age often have a comfort gesture involving hand contact with their mouth. It's nothing to worry about and shows you that your child feels relaxed and happy with things at the moment.

– hands clasped in front of him: this is usually a sign of tension, perhaps when he is being reprimanded or giving a minor public display. Clasped hands allows your child literally to hold his own hand, providing himself with reassurance and comfort in the face of stress.

– hand stroking chin gently: he is ready to make a decision about something, such as what drink to have or which biscuit to eat. Stroking his chin helps him think more clearly, so that he can weigh up the pros and cons of each alternative.

Leg Movements

Now that your growing child is fully mobile, having learned to walk and having shed the earlier 'puppy' fat that restricted his leg movements, he has a variety of leg gestures available to him, each of which is part of his non-verbal communication.

Common leg gestures that are often used by children at this age include:

– standing, but shifting from one foot to the other: this probably means that he's bored and wants a change of scenery. His frustration is building up – do something to ease it before he becomes irritable.

– legs crossed, while sitting on a chair: he is relaxed, at ease with himself, especially if this position is taken while watching television or during a chat with you or his friends. Even though he switches his upper and lower legs from time to time, he's not nervous; he feels good.

– legs crossed, but combined with crossed arms: this is one of the most aggressive, defiant gestures a child can make without actually saying a word. The aggression is emphasized if his facial expression bears a tight frown.

– standing, scratching the back of one leg absent-mindedly with his other foot: he is embarrassed about something but doesn't want to admit it. This gesture can also mean he's confused and isn't sure what course of action to take.

– sitting on the floor or on the edge of a chair, with

legs splayed wide open: he wants a bit of personal space at the moment. His splayed legs are the 'keep away' sign for anyone who might have thought about sitting beside him.

– kicking, or pushing hard with his feet: although this could be a playful action, the chances are that it is an unmistakable gesture of hostility, providing a direct release of his inner rage. Your child's kick may be directed at another child or at an object.

Touch

The most intimate action we can take is to touch another person. Touch is a primitive gesture that signifies care and affection, right from the moment of birth. Instinctively, a mother wants to hold her baby the first time she sees him, and breastfeeding depends entirely on touch between mother and child. Even when a baby is bottle-fed, he is held closely by his parents. Innate reflexes are often triggered by touch. For instance, when a finger is the placed in the palm of your new baby's hand, you'll discover that his fingers automatically close round it, gripping it tightly. And if his cheek is gently stroked, he'll immediately turn toward that direction.

As your child develops during the pre-school years, touch remains a vital part of his emotional satisfaction, but it is expressed in different ways. He wants to hold your hand when you go out together, he clings tightly to you when he's afraid, and he likes to sit on your knee for a cuddle when he's tired or when he's watching television. Play with his friends often involves bodily contact – young children adore rough-and-tumble play partly for this reason. Your child's need for this type of contact, however, diminishes as he grows older. By the time he is 13 or 14 years old, touch is almost exclusively reserved for specific family occasions (such as a hug from a distant relative, or from his sister on his birthday) or in the context of a budding romantic relationship. But in the meantime, touch is a two-way channel for him to communicate and receive emotions.

Personality affects the need for touch. Think about the children (and adults) you know. Some use touch a lot in any interaction with you (a handshake when seeing you, a light contact on the shoulder when saying goodbye, a peck on the cheek accompanying their congratulations on your birthday). Other people you know are less expressive physically and don't use touch in such an obvious way (such as those who say goodbye without making bodily contact, or who just say 'well done' rather than accompanying this with a pat on the back). It's a matter of personality – in most instances there is no connection between a child's innate feelings of warmth, love and cooperation and the amount of physical touch he uses.

And, like everyone, your child has a right to decide when he wants to be touched and when he doesn't. The choice must be his. In some instances, a young child has bodily contact forced upon him unwillingly by an adult, for instance when an aunt who hasn't seen him for a long time smothers him with kisses. Of course, this contact is benign and evolves from love, nothing more, but that doesn't mean he should have to accept it openly if it makes him feel uncomfortable. All children need to be given the confidence needed to say 'no' to unwelcome bodily contact.

Here are some situations in which your child may use touch or bodily contact to communicate his ideas and feelings:

– kisses you on the cheek: he feels affectionate towards you. Every parent loves their child to make this type of spontaneous gesture because it is such a primitive demonstration of love – but it doesn't mean he's rejecting you if he doesn't give you kisses all the time!

– leaning against you while you sit and read or watch television: he wants to be beside you because he feels very comfortable with you at that time. He might even sprawl all over you without actually realizing what he is doing.

– holding your hand: this gesture has different meanings depending on the other components of his body language (for example, it can mean terror if he is tense, it can mean pleasure if he is smiling and relaxed, it can mean enthusiasm if he pulls you in a specific direction).

– pushing you away: along with other touch gestures such as slapping, hitting and scratching, this is a sign of his aggression and anger. It is an instinctive reaction that combines both defence and attack.

– cuddling into you: he could be happy to be with you, but this form of contact might also mean that he is afraid or insecure. He may also feel sorry for himself as a result of something that happened earlier. Look at the rest of his body language and ask him about his day.

Summary

From the age of 3 and older, your child's use of body language becomes more sophisticated and starts to resemble that of adults. You have to work harder to interpret his non-verbal communication. The main channels of body language at this age include facial expression, body distance, body posture, eye movements, hand and arm gestures, leg movements and touch.

Chapter Five

What Your
Child Says to You

In this phase of your child's life she improves the skills she already has and develops new ones. In terms of physical changes, she grows approximately 5 or 7.5 cm (2 or 3 inches) every year, so that by the age of 6 she has reached almost two-thirds of what will be her adult height. She becomes thinner; her bones become stronger, muscle size increases, and her jaw broadens in preparation for the arrival of her second – and permanent – set of teeth. Brain growth is slower, but it will be almost adult size by the time she is 6 years old.

Coordination skills steadily improve during this phase of your child's life. Her leg and arm movements are more controlled, more graceful, less clumsy – this increases her ability to transmit non-verbal communication. Her social skills advance too, and she becomes more interested in playing with others. Solitary play is no longer attractive, as her need to play with other children her own age becomes paramount. Her social awareness heightens; she wants to be accepted by her friends so that she can play with them and join in their games. It is at this age that she starts to learn about turn-taking, sharing and cooperation, skills that are essential for her to be able to mix successfully with other children at her age and stage of development. Friendships are formed now, although these tend to be very superficial and may change from day to day, or even hour to hour. By the time she's 6, however, your child's friendships become more long-lasting.

The start of infant school is another major event in her life during this period. She loves educational games (such as sorting objects by shape, colour, etc.) and likes problem-solving activities (jigsaw puzzles and word games). The foundation for her later success at school is laid down in this period.

Her ability to use her imagination also becomes more controlled. She can use her imagination to think about experiences that have happened in the past, or that haven't even happened at all. She's no longer tied to the here and now, like she was when she was a toddler. You'll notice that she engages in fantasy play (imaginative play) a great deal now, and she particularly enjoys role-play with her friends and pretending to be someone else.

Emotions of a Young Child

The chart below lists the major emotional dimensions of your child's life between the ages of 3 and 6 years, and looks at ways these are most commonly expressed. Each of these dimensions affects your child's body language.

Child's Emotion	How It Is Expressed
Separation	She probably starts playgroup or nursery around the age of 3. This is a challenge for her and she needs to learn to cope on her own without having you beside her all the time.
Achievement	Around the age of 5, she starts school. This is the beginning of a major transition in her life. She wants to succeed and to do at least as well as her friends and classmates.
Excitement	Her inquiring and expanding mind means that she seeks excitement and challenge more than ever before. She'll be keen to try out new experiences, even if there are potential hazards involved.
Insecurity	Despite her successes, there will be plenty of times when her performance isn't what she had hoped it would be. This knocks her confidence badly and can lead to insecurity.
Friendliness	Peer-group relationships become very important. Through them, your child learns about herself and how to interact with others her own age. She starts to compare herself with her friends.

Loving   One of the ironies of this phase of
                      development is that the more your
                      child breaks away from you, the more
                      she needs to be in a close, loving rela-
                      tionship with you. Her connection
                      with you strengthens.

Recognizing Your Child's Emotions Through Body Language

Separation

During this phase of your child's life she begins to experience short, temporary separations from you, as when
she attends playgroup or nursery, or when she stays
with a childminder or babysitter. The chances are that
she will not enjoy these times away from you at first,
though she'll gradually get used to them. Until that stage
of confidence is reached, however, your child will want
to stay by your side at all times.

*Here are five ways your child uses body language to tell
you 'I know this activity will be fun, but I don't want to go
without you':*

1 **rubs tummy as if it is sore.** Her anxiety may show in
  the form of a sore tummy or a headache. The pain she
  feels is very real, even though the underlying cause is
  psychological rather than physical. You may find, for
  example, that she mentions these ailments to you the
  night before she is due to start at nursery.

2 **passive withdrawal and lethargy.** You would expect her to be ebullient and excited at the prospect of meeting new children and having a new range of activities. If her manner conveys the exact opposite – standing round-shouldered, head facing the ground – this is because she dreads the thought of leaving you.

3 **grips your hand tightly on the way to nursery.** Fear of the unknown makes her afraid, and when she is afraid she doesn't want to let go of you. Of course, she sometimes holds your hand tightly when she is happy, but the chances are that, if she is on her way to the childminder, nursery or school, she is anxious about it.

4 **slow to get dressed.** When she wakes full of anticipation for something later that morning, you can be sure she'll be out of bed and fully dressed, bright and early. Her natural enthusiasm makes her behave this way. However, any sluggishness or lack of desire to hurry tells you that she's in no rush to start her new day.

5 **tense facial expression.** By now, you know her well enough to recognize when her smile is a genuine one of pleasure, and when it masks underlying anxiety. Look for signs that her smile isn't real, such as her head tilting forward, mouth and eye muscles very tense, and her hand pulling nervously at her ear.

Tips for Responding to Your Child's Fear of Separation

Tell her in advance that you won't be with her for part of the day in question – she needs time to prepare herself psychologically for this difficult challenge. In addition, she will lose trust in you if you suddenly spring the separation on her. Whether or not she has difficulty coping with these separations from you, reassure her that she will be happy and safe when you are not with her. This reassurance helps calm her. And of course, stay calm yourself – worry is contagious, especially between parent and child, so you need to appear at ease or else your child will become agitated.

Make a point of reminding her that you are going to collect her at the end of the activity. This may seem obvious to you, but it might not be obvious to your child. Explain that you will be back soon, and return on time to avoid her having to stand around feeling lonely. Whether a childminder or nursery, a leisure class or a friend's house, talk to your child about the activity after you've brought her home again. Your interest and enthusiasm in the day's events will make her feel positive about it as well, and this in turn will increase her confidence for coping with the next separation.

Achievement

The start of infant school is one of the most significant transition phases in your child's life. No longer in an informal pre-school environment, your child is expected to conform to group standards of behaviour, to work cooperatively with others, to listen to what her teacher says, and to respond positively. Academic achievements become important. The new range of educational activities involved in literacy and numeracy place her in a competitive situation, possibly for the first time in her young life. She compares her progress and attainments with those of the other children in her infant class – and if they don't match up, her self-image will take a dive. Every child wants to do well at school.

Here are five ways your child uses body language to tell you 'I'm not feeling good because I can't keep up with the work in my class':

1 **spends a disproportionate amount of time on 'homework'.** An infant pupil who thinks she isn't doing as well as the others in her class will either spend too much time studying at home (that is, a lot more than 5 or 10 minutes) or won't show any interest at all. This is a clear message that she is floundering.

2 **refuses to talk about school.** Although some children are less communicative than others, you should expect your child to give you at least a brief account of her daily programme at school. Her reluctance to tell you about it, or her attempts to change the subject, should ring warning bells – the chances are her achievements are less than she hoped for.

3 **reluctance to participate in leisure activities.** Lack of achievement in school will reduce your child's confidence in other areas of her life, too; often there is a knock-on effect. Suddenly you'll discover that she doesn't want to go along to that dancing class she's been attending happily for years until now.

4 **easily frustrated.** Your child is quicker to lose her temper than she was before she started school. One

minute she's settled, the next minute her face is tight, her fists are clenched and she's stomping around the room angrily. Although this seems an extreme reaction to a trivial incident, it is a sign of her deeper dissatisfaction with herself.

5 **loses school-related objects.** Instead of keeping her school bag intact, with her pencils, notebooks and books all neatly arranged, you realize that she constantly loses her pencils or doesn't have the right notebook with her when she sets out in the morning. This is her way of letting you know that she's struggling to cope.

Tips for Responding to Your Child's Anxiety about Achieving

The first step is to let your child know that you are aware of the situation. She hasn't told you in spoken language because she either doesn't realize this is why she is unhappy or she is too embarrassed to say anything. But she is trying to tell you non-verbally. So speak to her directly about it. Ask her how she is getting on in school, how she feels about the work in the classroom, and so on. She may be reluctant initially to talk to you, but she'll become more open eventually. Sharing her feelings with you makes her feel better. Remind her that there are plenty of other children in her class who aren't finding school easy, even though she may not be aware of their difficulty.

The next step is to help her with the areas she is struggling with. If it is reading, then organize some reading materials for her at home. You'll probably want to speak to your child's teacher about this. Don't go overboard with extra work at home, however – a few minutes each night is all that is required for a child of 5 or 6.

Reassure her that her achievements will improve in the future. Tell her that now you know what she is worried about, you are sure that you'll be able to change things together. Your statement of support will be a big confidence-booster. Keep taking her along to any other extra-curricular classes she goes to, despite her temporary reluctance. Achievements in these non-academic areas of her life will compensate for lack of achievement at school.

Excitement

Now that she's older she is more confident in her ability to cope with new experiences. Her levels of excitement are high and her threshold for excitement is easily triggered. Your child hasn't yet got the maturity to recognize that she needs to be more circumspect when approaching a new activity, that she needs to assess every aspect before launching headlong into it. So when she wants to play with roller boots, she doesn't pause to consider the potential hazards such as people on the pavements, cars in the street, and so on. As far as your child is concerned, the world's one big adventure playground, a huge theme park, and she wants to try out everything she can immediately without waiting. Her increased reasoning skills and coordination skills means that she's ready and willing for anything.

It's not easy for you to curb her youthful excitement and enthusiasm.

Here are five ways your child uses body language to tell you 'I'm excited and can't wait much longer':

1 **shifts from one foot to the other, tapping her hands against her thighs.** This is one of the clearest signs of excitement. She appears restless, fidgets a lot, and her general body movements are sporadic and active. Her appetite may even drop dramatically as the excitement builds up, even though her appetite is usually good.

2 **eyes wide open, mouth partially open.** Have no doubt that this look on her face is telling you that she is thoroughly looking forward to whatever is coming next. In addition, her arms will be unfolded and her legs will be uncrossed. If seated, she'll probably lean forward on her chair.

3 **face downcast, eyes screwed up, body tense.** The anticipation may be so great that it actually makes your child appear anxious – but excitement can have this effect on a young child. She may start to cry, as though she is upset or afraid, when in fact the excitement has simply become too much for her.

4 **launches into a new activity without asking questions.** The prospect of the new bicycle, or getting into the swimming pool, reduces her interest in other aspects of the activity which she regards as trivial. This lack of questioning or discussion might lead you to think she is bored – she's not, though, just too excited to ask.

5 **calm, controlled and starts to organize her environment.** One way of coping with excitement is to focus on another activity altogether, one that requires your attention to detail. That's why you may discover your child busy tidying her toys or organizing her books, when you expect her to be bubbly and dynamic.

Tips for Responding to Your Child's Excitement

The enthusiasm and anticipation of a young child can be draining for parents, especially if they don't share the same feelings! Yet bear in mind that, although the activity or event may be quite routine for you, it probably isn't routine for your child. Instead of trying to limit her excitement, join in with it, if possible, letting her know how pleased you are that she is having such fun. On the other hand, there's no point in letting her get so worked up with excitement that the threshold of enjoyment is breached. Laughter can soon turn into tears with a child this age. Try to calm her, without forcing her to lose the positive mood altogether. You want her to have fun, but you don't want her to lose control of her feelings altogether.

If you see her level of excitement building up to the point where a crisis may develop, sit her down and give her something to do. She'll resist, naturally, because all her instincts tell her to move around energetically. But encourage her into a more sedate activity anyway. This provides her with a strategy to use in the future. And talk to her about the activity: this shows her you are happy for her to be excited about it, while still keeping her from getting too physically or emotionally worked up about it.

Insecurity

Your child's sense of security is so fragile at this age; all it takes is a minor argument or failure at some trivial task in order to rock her self-confidence and make her feel insecure. Psychological research confirms that a child who is lacking in self-confidence tends to do less well at school than would be expected on the basis of her intellectual ability, and has greater difficulty making new friends with other children her own age. She needs your help and support to make her feel more secure.

Here are five ways your child uses body language to tell you 'I'm feeling insecure and I don't have much trust in my own abilities':

1 **reluctance to play with her friends.** Her feelings of insecurity reduce her pleasure in being with other children her own age. She doesn't feel safe with them and would prefer to be at home. Your suggestion that she play with another child is met with a sullen response, and a total lack of interest in the whole idea.

2 **disparaging attitude towards herself.** Nothing she does is valued by her. Instead of keeping a drawing or painting that she has just completed, she screws it up and throws it straight into the bin. She doesn't feel secure enough to show what she has made to anyone else, for fear of rejection.

3 **becomes afraid when new activities are suggested.**

When you explain to your child that you would like her to take up a new leisure activity such as a musical instrument, she visibly shrinks at the idea. Her face screws up, her shoulders tighten, and she may even step back from you.

4 **tears and tension when leaving you.** She doesn't want to let go of you when, for instance, you take her to nursery or to school. However, don't make the mistake of assuming that she's afraid of something that is going on there – her body language is saying that she feels insecure about being on her own.

5 **lack of enthusiasm and general apathy.** Along with other emotions, feelings of insecurity can lead your child to act in a disinterested, almost lazy, manner. This sluggishness in her body movements and bore-dom in her facial expression can be a non-verbal way of telling you that she is insecure.

Tips for Responding to Your Child's Insecurity

A child of this age of feels terribly insecure when facing new challenges because she lacks confidence in her own ability to cope. However, she is probably more capable than she thinks – she just needs to experience success in order to prove to herself that she can manage. If, for instance, she is worried because she knows there will be a colouring-in activity at nursery the next day and that she is not good at this, let her practise at home the day before. This reduces her insecurity. And point out her strengths and talents to her.

Friendliness

Friendships matter now, more than ever before. Through relationships with others your child learns a great deal about herself, her characteristics, and her strengths and weaknesses. She may be very sensitive, afraid of rejection and convinced that others don't like her, or she may be so confident that the hurtful remarks of others just bounce off her. Whatever your child's personality is, she wants to be liked, and will be unhappy if she feels excluded from her peer group.

Here are five ways your child uses body language to tell you 'I enjoy playing with others and would like to have more friends':

1 **tears when she comes home from school or nursery.** The one thing that is guaranteed to make your child feel miserable is not receiving an invitation to a birthday party which all her friends have been invited to. If she does come home crying, talk to her gently until she reveals the true reason.

2 **involves herself in busy preparations before a friend comes to the house.** Watch how she behaves in the hour or two before her friend is due to visit. A degree of preparation – such as tidying her room – lets you know that she anticipates having a good time and wants everything to be ready for her friend.

3 **reduces the body distance between herself and other children.** You'll notice that she places herself closer to other children, including those whom she doesn't know very well, so that they virtually have to

include her in their activities. The normal circle of personal space is reduced to allow friendships to form.

4   **bodily contact with other children her own age.** Friendship at all ages can be expressed through touch, although this form of contact is particularly common up to the age of 5 or 6 years. Your child might hold her friend's hand when they play together, or they might hug each other spontaneously.

5   **improved eye-contact.** A young child instinctively knows to gaze into others' eyes if she wants to be friendlier with them. Look at the level of eye-contact your child makes when she is with others; she'll make it more frequently, and hold it for longer, when she is with a child she especially likes.

Tips for Responding to Your Child's Need for Friends

You can help your child make friends more easily by helping her communicate effectively using both body language and spoken language. Misunderstandings between children of this age often stem from a child's inability to communicate her feelings and ideas clearly. If your child learns to express her feelings by saying 'I like you and I would like to sit beside you' or by simply smiling and sitting beside the other child while doing so, then she is less likely to be rejected than if she plonks herself down on the chair with a blank expression on her face and without saying a word. Encourage her to be more communicative so that other children understand her intentions.

At some point during play your child will be asked to share her toys; if she is unwilling to do this other children will reject her. Teach her how to share by explaining why she should do this and by example. Similarly, she needs to learn how to take turns when playing a game, and also how to follow the rules of a game.

Loving

Your child needs to be loved – this need is both permanent and vital. A child who isn't loved will fail to thrive. Right from birth she needs you to hold her lovingly, to care for her and stimulate her. And this need for love never changes. True, it may be expressed differently as your child develops, but it is always there. Sometimes she will appear so grown up to you – even a child aged 4 or 5 can seem mature compared to when she was younger – yet she continues to need your love.

Here are five ways your child uses body language to tell you 'I may be a big girl now but I still need lots of love':

1 **cuddles you before going out to play.** You may be surprised to see such a spontaneous demonstration of her need for love, as you were probably expecting her to dash out without saying a word to you. This unexpected show of emotion through bodily contact is an expression of this emotional need.

2 **insists that you read her a bedtime story.** Now that she can read, she really doesn't depend on you so much for a story at bedtime – she can read it herself. Her insistence that you continue with this practice

95

tells you that she still needs a close emotional relationship with you.

3 **brings you into her intimate circle of body space.**
While watching television with you and the rest of her family, you suddenly realize that she is snuggled up close to you, having allowed you into the intimate circle of personal space around her. This action, coupled with the bodily contact, is an expression of her continued need for bonding.

4 **shares her news with you.** At the end of a hard day, you'll possibly have little energy left to listen to your young child's tales – you may even find her constant chattering intrusive. However, this is her way of telling you that she still needs you and that she still gets pleasure from talking to you about the events of her life.

5 **relaxes in your presence.** Observe your child's general manner when she's with you. She appears calm, her face, arm and leg muscles are relaxed, and she is very much at ease. Her head may be slightly tilted backwards and she laughs at even the slightest joke you make. When sitting in a chair, she'll sag into it rather than take an upright pose.

Tips for Responding to Your Child's Need for Love

Some parents assume that signs of affection are best left behind at the toddler stage of development, and that when a child reaches school age she no longer should need a kiss or a hug – and certainly not in public. Outward demonstrations of love through bodily contact may be discouraged, as they are seen as signs of immaturity. This is a pity. There's no law that says there is a specific age when a child should stop being hugged. If she has a continued need to do this, then let her. It's not going to cause your child (or you!) any harm.

Take an interest in your child's activities and encourage her to talk to you about them. Your interest makes her feel that she matters to you. Similarly, comfort her when she is upset. Naturally you want her to develop personal strength so that she doesn't need to come running to someone every time something goes wrong, but she's not yet ready to be entirely independent. She needs your comfort, love and reassurance, and has a right to expect them from you.

Summary

Massive changes take place in your child's development between the ages of 3 and 6. She changes physically, intellectually, socially and emotionally, and these changes show in the way she uses body language. The main emotional dimensions in her life at this stage include fear of separation from you, the need to make positive achievements in school, the desire for excitement, a sense of insecurity, a desire to increase her friendships, and a need to maintain a loving relationship with you. Each dimension is reflected in her non-verbal communication.

Part Four

Body Language
Matters

Chapter Six

When Things Go Wrong

No matter how well-behaved your child is, or how even-tempered he is, there will be times when life does not go according to plan. The way he communicates this to you will vary, depending on the specific circumstances and on the perceived outcomes:

– **open admission.** In some instances, your child may tell you outright about the situation (such as that he was cheeky to his class teacher and is now very upset about it). Although you won't be too pleased to hear such news, his spoken language gives you all the information you need; you can then take action accordingly.
– **partial admission.** In some instances your child may be reluctant to give you a full account of what has happened, and instead may only tell you part of the story (he reveals that he has had a disagreement with his friend, but fails to mention that he himself

started it). His body language will tell you there is more to the story than he has told you verbally.

– **lying.** In some instances your child may know that he has done something wrong but may then deliberately choose to hide the truth from you, in order to escape the consequences (such as when he denies responsibility for the mess in the sitting room). His body language will show you that he is telling a lie.

– **concealment through fear.** There may be occasions when your child deliberately conceals information from you, not because he is afraid of punishment but because he is embarrassed or humiliated and fears that telling you will only exacerbate the situation (such as when he is bullied or abused). His body language will give this away.

– **genuine denial.** In some instances, your child will be troubled and unhappy, even though he doesn't know why – and may not actually realize he is unhappy. You will need to pick up on his non-verbal cues in order to learn about his true feelings.

Understanding Your Child When He is Troubled

So interpreting your child's non-verbal communication is vital for detecting when he is in trouble, for detecting when he is deliberately trying to conceal information from you, and for detecting when something is troubling him.

Open Admission

Although you may be more concerned with reading your child's body language in order to identify whether or not he's concealing something from you, it's still worth while recognizing the body language he uses when he is telling the truth – this may avert misunderstandings, and in turn reduce the amount or frequency of unnecessary accusations and confrontations between you.

Here are five ways your child uses body language to tell you 'I'm telling you the truth and I want you to believe me':

1 **strong eye-contact.** His confidence will be strong because he knows he is telling the truth, even though you may not like what he says. He is able to look you straight in the eye when talking to you. Even if you challenge his account, he can still maintain good eye-contact with you.

2 **eyes wide open.** Instinctively, he'll open his eyes wider than he does during normal speech, as part of his attempt to convince you his words are authentic. In addition, his eyebrows will probably be slightly raised, and the lower part of his brow slightly furrowed – he is intent that you believe him.

3 **good body posture.** The normal tell-tale signs of meekness, such as sagging shoulders and hanging his head, are absent when your child tells the truth. Your child's shoulders will be held high, his back will be straight and he will stand facing you square on. His whole posture gives an impression of self-confidence.

4 **positive response.** Your child will give a very positive reaction when he realizes that you believe him. Whereas a child who is lying will probably heave a sigh of relief when he thinks his story has been believed, the reaction of a child telling the truth will be one of obvious pleasure.

5 **gives you a hug.** Don't forget that he is still a young child and many of his emotional responses remain spontaneous. So when you announce that you believe him, he may well rush forward and give you a huge cuddle – he's upset that you may have doubted him but is reassured that you now believe him.

How to React to an Open Admission

The most important reaction you can have to your child's honesty – even though you may be upset by what he has told you – is pleasure and encouragement. He needs this in order to reinforce the correctness of his actions. Tell him how pleased you are that he has told you the truth, that you know how difficult it must have been for him, and that you always want him to tell you the truth in future, no matter what he has done.

If the information he has told you requires some action from him or from you, then offer him suggestions. Your solutions to his difficulty will be welcome, and will help the two of you to develop mutual trust. Of course, you may be angry about what he has told you – if so, you should certainly reprimand him, but make sure your reprimand isn't so severe that he is discouraged from being honest with you the next time. Always try to end any reproach on a positive note.

Partial Admission

There will undoubtedly have been times when you've wanted to tell your partner about an incident that happened to you during the day, but have been reluctant to tell the full story – perhaps because you have been embarrassed or because you've worried that your partner would not react in the way you want. Say for example that while you were out shopping someone barged ahead of you in the supermarket queue; your objection was probably so mild, and the person who barged in front so obnoxious, that you eventually decided not to complain to the person about it. By the time you are back home, however, you are annoyed at having been put upon and also annoyed because you did not take any effective action. So you tell your partner about the first part (that is, that someone jumped the queue) but not about the second part (that is, you let it happen without doing anything to stop it).

Most people find themselves in a situation like this at one time or another – in other words, they experience an incident that they are not keen to explain fully to another person. Your child is no different from you in this respect. He wants to appear capable and important in your eyes, so that he will gain your full approval and confidence. Certainly he doesn't want to feel miserable about something that has occurred, and then have that misery compounded by your unhelpful criticism and disapproval of his actions. So he only tells you half the story.

Here are five ways your child uses body language to tell you 'I've only told you half of what I should because I'm a bit embarrassed about what happened':

1 **open mouth once he has finished speaking.** This is an involuntary action; unconsciously he wants to tell you more but stops himself. So his mouth remains open for a few moments, as though he intends to say more. You may even notice that he silently mouths a couple of words which you can't make out clearly.

2 **restless after he has told you.** Because there is more that he really wants to tell you, he feels restless. Even if he stays seated, you'll observe that he moves around a lot, adjusting his position every few seconds. This is a demonstration of his discomfort.

3 **furrowed brow.** His eyebrows may be raised, his brow furrowed and his eyes opened quite wide. This type of facial expression usually accompanies a feeling of disbelief and occurs at this time because your child knows that what he is telling you isn't the entire truth. Just by looking, you'll know he wants to tell you more.

4 **stays beside you.** Your child's normal reaction when he has finished talking to you is to turn his attention to another activity, and possibly to move away from you. However, when he has something else that he wants to say yet is reluctant to say it, he may stay beside you, prompting you to ask him if there is anything else troubling him.

5 taps his hands nervously. The drumming of fingers against the side of a chair,, or the tapping of hands against his thighs, is a sure sign that he has more he wants to communicate verbally. He'll probably throw regular glances in your direction as well, just to confirm to himself that he is attracting your attention.

How to React to a Partial Admission

The main thing to remember is that your child desperately wants to tell you his problem – the strategy of holding back information is used to protect himself from further distress. This means that directly challenging him is not the way forward. For instance, saying 'I know there's more to it than this. Just tell me what else happened' or 'There's no point in hiding things from me, I'll find out sooner or later' will force him to react defensively and to pretend that he does not understand what you are saying to him.

It is far better to take a gentle, sympathetic approach, so that he realizes further disclosure will not be greeted with a negative reaction from you. For instance, you may want to say to him, 'You seem troubled; maybe there is something else I can help you with' or 'Sometimes I'm embarrassed about an incident that happened to me but I always find I feel better when I tell someone about it.' Statements such as these convey your desire for him to share his emotions with you, creating an atmosphere conducive to honest communication between parent and child.

Loving physical contact may also help him relax. Put

your arm around him, or let him sit on your knee – this body language tells him that you care for him, and this may be sufficient to encourage him to tell you everything.

Listen to what he has to say; offer advice where possible. Explain to him that you always want him to tell you about anything that upsets him, and that he'll feel better for doing so. Once he realizes that he can reveal difficult and potentially disturbing accounts to you without arousing your anger or disapproval in return, then he may be more open with you in future. Of course, there may be instances when his disclosure requires you to punish him in some way because he has misbehaved. But make sure he realizes you are still pleased he was direct and honest with you, even though you didn't like what he said.

Deliberate Concealment (Lying)

Almost certainly there will be times when your child deliberately conceals information from you – lying is common among young children. Remember, though, that there is a difference between a child's lie and an adult's lie. An adult who tells lies knows the full moral and practical implications of such an action, whereas the same cannot always be said of a young child. So when you catch your child telling a lie, don't over-react. Before punishing him, think about why he might have tried to conceal the truth.

Most lies in childhood are motivated by fear of discovery. The chances are that your child did not deliberately do something wrong – but once he realizes his action was unacceptable, his natural instinct is to conceal the truth. And if his terror of punishment is so extreme, he'll work hard at maintaining the lie in the face of your enquiries. A young child has an amazing capacity to insist his version of events is accurate, even though the evidence does not support him. For example, you may notice that the area around his mouth is smeared with chocolate, yet he'll vigorously deny being responsible for the missing sweets. You'll probably discover that the more you press him to tell the truth, the more he sticks to his original story; soon you may become so confused that you don't know what to think. His nonverbal communication will be one of the best indicators of whether or not he is telling the truth.

Here are five ways your child uses body language to tell you 'I'm not telling the truth but I hope you will believe me':

1 **failure to make eye-contact.** His fear of discovery, coupled with the fact that he almost certainly doesn't like having to lie to you, results in his inability to look you straight in the eye. Ask him to look at you when you talk to him – if he isn't telling the truth, then you'll see him turn his eyes away nervously.

2 **discomfort.** Look for signs that he is uncomfortable. For instance, he might be very restless and want to move around while explaining the situation to you, or he might wring his hands tightly together as you speak to him. Any body movements that suggest anxiety and tension could indicate he is aware that he is lying to you.

3 **red cheeks.** From the age of 2 or 3 onwards he'll know that it is wrong to lie to you and he'll feel guilty about it. This will make his cheeks go red. He can't control this emotional reaction – a rush of blood to the face when you question him strongly suggests he is lying.

4 **nervous gestures.** Even a child who is generally calm will often develop distinctive gestures when telling a lie. The mannerisms to look for include repetitive comfort gestures, such as stroking his ear lobe again and again or rubbing his eye furiously, or slight facial tics, such as a twitching eyebrow or trembling lip.

5 **covering-up actions.** A child who doesn't like lying – and most children hate it – may try literally to 'cover-up' while giving the false account. For instance, he might mumble incoherently so that his words can't be heard, or he might inadvertently cover his mouth with his hand as he speaks. The meaning of these actions is unmistakable.

How to React to Lying

It is entirely up to you how you respond to the knowledge that your child has lied to you. But remember that, if your reaction is too extreme, he'll be even more afraid of discovery the next time and he'll try even harder to conceal the true version of events from you.

Of course you may feel you have to punish him in some way, and of course you must make him understand that such behaviour is simply not acceptable. Yet you should also bear in mind that a young child doesn't see the world in the same way that you do. For instance, you know that a child who tells lies persistently will inevitably be rejected by his peers and by other adults because nobody trusts a liar, and you may well be terrified of this happening to your child. However, he is unlikely to think that far ahead. As far as your child is concerned, lying is an immediate way of avoiding trouble, that's all.

Tell your child that you can always tell when he is lying because of the look on his face (even if you can't, he will still believe you and this acts as a deterrent in the future). Explain fully the reasons why you think lying is unacceptable (you will not know when to trust him and when not to, his friends won't want to play with him, etc.) and encourage him to tell you the truth always, despite the fact that you may disapprove of what he has to tell you. Try to avoid creating a climate of fear, in which the dread of telling the truth outweighs the fear of telling a lie, otherwise lying will always be your child's first alternative. Repeat this message again and again. For instance, you could say 'I always want you to tell the truth even though I may be angry with you. I'll always prefer that to a lie.'

Punish his lies firmly and sensibly, while making sure your child understands that you still care for him. Punishment can range from a stern telling-off to an early bedtime; it really depends on you and your child. What suits one parent-child relationship may not suit another. Let your child know that once the incident is over, it genuinely is over – unless he chooses to start it up again by lying in the future. The next time he is in a tight spot and yet is honest with you, make a big fuss of him; that's the best way encourage honesty in the future.

Concealment through Fear

One of the reasons why bullying and other forms of abuse are allowed to persist is that the victim is usually too afraid to disclose any details of the punishment he has been receiving. The victim is embarrassed and humiliated by his own weakness, powerlessness and inability to take effective action himself. The weaker the victim, the stronger the bully.

Bullying in families (from sibling to sibling) or in school (from pupil to pupil) is much more common than most parents like to think. After all, no parents happily entertain the notion that their child is a bully. Although you may think of bullying in terms of direct physical violence, such as one child punching another, it can take many forms at home and at school, including:

- the use of hands: punching or slapping to the face or body, pushing, nudging or jostling, poking in the side or face, rude gestures
- the use of legs: violent kicking, deliberate tripping, kicking the victim's school bag or lunch box, stamping on his foot
- extortion: demanding money from a child, then threatening him with a beating if he doesn't cooperate fully with these demands
- verbal abuse: teasing a child about his appearance

or disability, using words to taunt him, threatening to
hurt him
– racial harassment: racially-motivated attacks,
either physical or psychological.

Although bullying is very real and obvious to the child
on the receiving end, it may not be obvious to his
parents. Often, a victim withstands bullying for several
months without saying anything about it, because he is
afraid that telling his parents will make the bully pick on
him even more or that he will look a fool. This is particularly true when the bullying is carried out by an older
brother or sister. The bully thrives through a reign of
terror.

*Here are five ways your child uses body language to tell
you 'I'm being bullied but I don't want to tell you':*

1 **partially hidden cuts and bruises.** Young children
   usually delight in showing off their cuts and bruises,
   as though they are signs of bravery. But a child who is
   bullied is more secretive about grazes and other abra-
   sions – when questioned about them, he will be
   evasive and will give unsatisfactory answers.
2 **fear of being alone.** After a while, a victim becomes
   afraid of his own company because he feels so vulnerable. So he insists on staying with his parents or with
   other children; this makes him feel more protected.
   Also, he may resist being left alone with a particular
   sibling if that child is the one who bullies him.
3 **loss of possessions.** As well as physical and verbal

abuse, bullies often take possessions from their victims because this is a further demonstration of their power. So a non-verbal sign of bullying is the repeated discovery that your child has lost his pencils, his school bag or his pocket money.

4 **wetting and soiling.** A child who has full bowel and bladder control and yet who suddenly starts to have incidents of wetting and soiling, may be being bullied. This behaviour can also derive from other causes of emotional stress, but bullying must be considered as a possibility. Only become concerned if these toilet accidents are frequent, however.

5 **worried facial expression.** Victims feel depressed, confused and afraid all the time. They see no end to their plight, and hence the down-trodden expression on their face. If your child is in this situation, you won't fail to notice his furrowed brow, his tight face muscles and his downward gaze.

How to React to Bullying

If you suspect that bullying is a possibility, be open with your child. Explain that you know some children are aggressive to others and that you think he might be a victim of such hostility. If he admits that he is being bullied, treat his comments seriously. Remember that it takes courage for your child to reveal the truth – he will be terrified in case the bully finds out he has spoken to you. Reassure him that it is a sign of strength, not weakness, to enlist your help, and that you see it as part of your role as a parent to defend him. Try to prevail upon him the importance of taking the matter up with his teacher, headmaster, or even the bully's parents. If he insists that you keep the matter confidential, however, assure him that you will – and keep your word.

Suggest that he keep out of the bully's way in the meantime, as that's one of the best ways to avoid being bullied. Unfortunately, children frequently have very stereotyped notions of bravery and mistakenly think that it is better to take a beating from a bully than to run away – it's up to you to convince your child otherwise. And encourage him to show as little reaction as possible. Teasing thrives when the victim reacts to it; indifference is a more effective response.

Certainly you should not tell him to fight back, as this strategy is fraught with potential hazards. For instance, he may end up with a severe beating. Or he may decide to be violent whenever another child annoys him. If the bullying occurs at school, suggest he stays in a crowd when in the playground. Bullies pick on children who appear weak and isolated – a child standing alone in a playground is easily identified as a potential target. Being with a crowd doesn't guarantee an undisturbed playtime, but it does make bullying less likely.

Genuine Denial

Like most children, your child is probably fortunate enough to feel happy most of the time. While he experiences instances of short-term unhappiness, these moments are transient – as when he becomes almost hysterical when you won't buy him a toy he fancies, yet forgets all about it by the evening. These minor bouts of unhappiness disappear as quickly as they arrive, without leaving any long-term scars. This is a normal part of childhood.

For some children, however, unhappiness is not temporary. The distress does not go away after a few minutes or hours, but instead stays without diminishing. There are two emotional characteristics that develop in a child who is generally unhappy and troubled. First, he may not realize that he is distressed. For him, the state of feeling miserable may be so routine that he regards this feeling as normal – the unhappiness is so pervasive that he doesn't remember a time when he felt differently. Secondly, even if he does realize that he is thoroughly miserable, he probably won't know what causes him to feel this way. He may have repressed the true source of his emotional pain into the unconscious part of his mind – when that happens, the feelings remain but the child has blocked out the reason for the feelings because he can't cope with it. There are many factors that can disturb a child's normal emotional development:

– fighting with his best friend. Friendships are always fragile in childhood, but that does not mean your child is content to stop playing with a child he previously liked a lot.
– struggling to complete assignments in school. Knowing that work in class is too challenging can be enough to depress any child.
– poor self-confidence. If your child doesn't feel good

about himself, then others won't like him either – and this will add to his misery and despair.

– fights between mum and dad. No matter what age your child is, he won't like to witness fights between you and your partner, whether these are overt or more subtle.

– abuse. A child who is physically, emotionally or sexually abused will appear troubled and unsettled. He will have great difficulty acknowledging that the abuse is happening, and may also prefer to remain silent about it.

Here are five ways your child uses body language to tell you 'I'm unhappy deep down inside, even though I've not said anything to you about it':

1 **reluctance to play with friends.** A child who is unhappy has difficulty both maintaining existing friendships and making new friends. He'll be unenthusiastic at the prospect of another child coming to play with him; if he is unwillingly put in that situation, then bickering may break out.

2 **loss of appetite.** Your appetite probably diminishes greatly when you are worried about something; meals that previously you would have relished suddenly are not so attractive. The same applies to your child. Although a decrease in appetite can indicate ill-health, it can also be a sign of desolation.

3 **general apathy.** Be concerned if you notice that your child gradually becomes listless and apathetic,

lounging about the house without his usual zest. As with appetite loss, this too can be a sign of illness. However, unhappiness has the effect of driving away a child's usual liveliness and sparkle.

4 **disrupted sleeping patterns.** An unhappy child will not sleep well. He'll have trouble falling asleep to start with, and he'll wake up regularly throughout the night because he generally feels unsettled emotionally. Each morning when he gets up, he'll look like he is ready to go straight back to bed again.

5 **irritability.** There is a direct link between unhappiness and irritability. A child who feels miserable won't have the patience to listen to others or to tolerate their presence. His temper will be triggered easily and he'll be ready to fly off the handle without much provocation. In reality, however, the child's anger is directed at himself.

How to React to Genuine Denial

Where you suspect that your child's body language reveals he is deeply unhappy, the first step should be to ask him outright if there is anything troubling him. His most likely answer will be that he can't think of anything, that he isn't unhappy at all and that he just feels slightly unwell most of the time. However, talk to him about the key areas in his life, such as friendships, leisure activities, school and so on. Perhaps through a general discussion like this he'll gain some insight into his underlying feelings.

Once you have spent some time considering the

possible circumstances that could be troubling him – although you won't be certain you are right – talk to other people who know your child, to ascertain their views. This could be your child's nursery nurses or his teacher, your older children, or one of your friends who knows him well. Listen to what they have to say, even though your initial reaction might be to disagree with them.

Put these points to him, in a way that he will understand. His reaction might be to dismiss your suggestions outright, saying that there is nothing wrong with him. On the other hand, you might hit the nail on the head at the very start and discover that he bursts into tears at one of the suggestions you make. Either way, your efforts to discuss this with your child reminds him that you care for him and for his well-being, that he matters to you, and that you want him to be happy. This in itself is a positive step forward.

Once this information-gathering and discussion phase has passed, make some changes in your child's life. Do what you can to bring about gradual alterations to his daily life, and monitor the effect of these changes until you are satisfied he has settled down. For instance, if you think that he is unhappy because he has no friends, then enrol him in a leisure class or invite a couple of children his age over to the house to play with him. Or if you think he has a problem keeping up with school work, talk to his class teacher, help him with his homework and give him lots of encouragement. If you are concerned that your child is unhappy because you and your partner have been arguing with each other a lot recently, reassure him that you both love him and that he is perfectly safe.

Summary

Every child has his 'ups and downs' in life, though he doesn't always want to talk to you about the 'downs'. In some instances he may only tell you half the truth, he might deliberately lie to you to avoid punishment, he might conceal information through embarrassment or he might not realize he is troubled. Whatever the circumstances, your child's body language will reveal that there is more to his story than he has told you in words. You can interpret your child's bodily language to enable you to get to the truth, and then to take supportive action where necessary.

Chapter Seven

Using Body Language Positively

In this book you have been encouraged to view body language as another way of understanding your child, another way of accessing her deeper emotions. Non-verbal communication transmits a great deal of information from child to parent, and therefore your enhanced knowledge of your child's body language can only benefit your relationship. The more understanding you have, then the greater the bond between you.

The Importance of First Impressions

This is not the only purpose of body language, however. Remember that your child also uses body language to communicate with people other than yourself. And the messages she gives can either be negative or positive. Suppose, when you meet a child for the first time, that she scowls at you, turns her back on you and huffs and puffs angrily. Suppose further that she ignores your comments, pushes you away and sticks her tongue out at you. There is no doubt you would form an adverse impression of this child, even though you didn't yet know her at all.

Now suppose you meet another child for the first time, only this child is smiling and attentive, and looks at you as she speaks to you. She offers you a sweet and has a sparkling expression on her face. There is no doubt you would form an positive impression of this child, even though you didn't really know her at all either.

Neither of these judgements is fair. After all, a few brief snatches of body language are hardly sufficient to reveal anyone's true nature. It's possible that you caught the first child on an 'off' day, and that she is normally more sociable and sensitive; or that the second child was putting on an act to fool you. But human nature is such that we judge by first impressions, no matter how hard we try not to. So if a child's body language is in any way negative, then others – whether children or adults – will quickly take a dislike to her. Fortunately, however, the converse is also true – a child with positive body language is much more likely to be viewed favourably at a first meeting.

It makes sense, therefore, for you to encourage your child to use body language deliberately in a way that will work in her favour. This is not teaching her to be devious, just practical. Popular children tend to be happier children; so your help with non-verbal communication can increase your child's chances of social success.

Action Plan

Here is a step-by-step plan for encouraging your child to use her body language so that she conveys a very positive first impression:

Step 1:	Identify the components of body language that are fundamental in fostering a favourable impression in the eyes of others. You need to be very clear on this so that you can emphasize the right ones.
Step 2:	Explain to your child that the way she behaves when meeting new children and adults will affect the way they behave towards her. A child as young as 3 or 4 will understand you when you tell her this.
Step 3:	Pick only one item of positive body language at a time to teach your child – you will, of course, extend this once her confidence grows, but in the first instance one aspect of non-verbal communication at a time is sufficient for a young child.
Step 4:	Show her by example. For instance, if you want her to face others square on, then stand her in a fixed position and face her in the pose you want her to adopt. Or you could have her stand beside you, modelling your actions.

Step 5:	Practise by using role-play. Your child will enjoy using her imagination in this type of activity. Pretend that you are a stranger and that she is meeting you for the first time. Role-play allows your child to practise these skills in a safe and reassuring environment.
Step 6:	Praise your child when she begins to use the positive body language that you have taught her. Tell her how pleased you are with her, and remind her that others will form a better first impression of her as a result of this.
Step 7:	Monitor your child's body language over the next few months to ensure that she continues to use it positively. You can also suggest she look for examples of positive body language in other children.

Body Language and First Impressions

Probably the most striking non-verbal dimension when you see a child for the first time is her **body posture**. You notice a person's body position from a distance, before you can see the expression on his or her face, and so it should be the first 'body language skill' for you to teach your child.

She may be shy by nature when she first meets an unfamiliar child or adult, and therefore develop a rather defensive body posture whenever she is in this situation, keeping her shoulders rounded and sloping towards the ground, her back rounded as well, her hands hanging limply by her side. Her legs may be slightly bent at the knees. In addition to this 'closed' body posture, she may turn her side or back to a stranger, making contact even less inviting. The whole impression of this stance is to say 'Keep away, I don't want to know you.'

All that is required are a few subtle changes in the way she stands in order for your child to make a much more positive impact on an unfamiliar child or adult. Her body posture should be more open, welcoming and altogether more assertive. Most importantly, she needs to stand upright, shoulders held square and upright as though she is leaning firmly against a wall. Likewise, her neck and head should also be held upright. The position of her hands becomes less important when the rest of her body posture is so positive, and so she has a choice of leaving her hands by her side or clasping them gently in front of her. Your child should face the stranger as the distance between them narrows, making eye-contact easier. A stance like this says 'I'm confident and I'm ready to meet you.'

The next most important dimension is **eye-contact**. The eyes are truly the 'windows to the soul', and direct eye-contact is a very welcoming component of body language. In fact, one of the reasons why babies are so appealing is because their eyes are disproportionately large in relation to the size of their head – and this adds to their attractiveness. It's only in later childhood that head growth reduces the relative size of the eyes.

Making positive eye-contact, however, is not a simple

matter. Eye-contact alone does not necessarily create a favourable impression. Simply telling your child to look into the other child's eyes when she meets him for the first time may be misread – the child might interpret this in a number of ways, some of which are negative, including:

- aggression: constant eye-contact can be construed as hostile, especially if it is accompanied by a frowning facial expression.
- disinterest: if the rest of your child's body language suggests she is disinterested, then fixed eye-contact will only confirm this.
- unfriendliness: unbroken eye-contact can be very disconcerting, unless there are other signs of sociability, such as a smiling face.

Explain to your child that there is a difference between making strong eye-contact and 'staring down' another child. Good eye-contact means looking the other child square in the eye, while occasionally looking away. (Unbroken eye-contact isn't comfortable to maintain or to receive, and usually suggests a more sinister emotion.) Certainly, eye-contact should always be made when talking to another person – this shows interest and concern.

Eye-contact becomes even more positive when it is accompanied by a **smiling facial expression**. The problem is that, when your child is nervous about meeting someone new, she will find it difficult – perhaps impossible – to force a smile onto her face. Her natural impulse is to tighten her facial muscles, especially those around her mouth, giving a tense expression. And nobody finds that inviting! Yet a smile is the most spontaneous way of showing pleasure in a greeting, and so you should encourage her to smile, even though this is the last thing she may feel like doing at that precise moment.

She can practise this at home, in front of the mirror. Suggest to your child that she face her reflection and look at her mouth. Encourage her to notice the line that her mouth takes when she doesn't smile – it'll be somewhat flat and her teeth won't be visible. Then get her to smile (perhaps by making a joke or even tickling her) and ask her to tell you the difference between her mouth when she's smiling and when she is not. This increases her self-awareness.

The next stage is for her to practise smiling while looking at herself in the mirror. If she finds this difficult, ask her to imagine that she sees the face of her best friend and that she should smile in response to that image. Children have very vivid imaginations and therefore are able to use imagery effectively in situations like this. The more your child practises smiling, the easier it becomes for her. Bear in mind that there is a difference between a genuine smile and a false smile – the eyes give it away. However, practice in smiling will mean that your child finds it easier to smile spontaneously when greeting an unfamiliar child or adult.

Lastly, your child should also try to be **relaxed** if she wants to create a positive first impression. Meeting new people is difficult for most children, and their natural reaction is for the muscles to tense. Tension shows itself in body language in a number of ways.

For instance, your child's facial muscles will contract, making the act of smiling a remote possibility. The muscles around her eyes will also tighten, making her eyes slightly narrower; her rate of blinking may also increase, indicating nervousness, and she may develop a slight facial tic. As well as that, her trunk and arm muscles appear inflexible and rigid, as though she can't bend at all or as though she is rooted to the spot. Again this will be interpreted as anxiety and tension. Her legs muscles also react in the same way, and she might feel the urge to move back and forth. You may have noticed when your child is nervous she shakes her leg, perhaps bending it at the knee, backwards and forwards – this is an involuntary reaction of which she is probably unaware. All these different aspects of body language generate a first impression that indicates tension and poor self-confidence.

As with most aspects of body language, your child can gain control over her feelings of tension by practising relaxation exercises at home. It is simply a matter of breath control and muscle control. There are many ways to teach relaxation (and you may have learned one or two techniques in your ante-natal classes). However, the following simple strategy is popular with children as it is easy to understand.

First, ensure your child is sitting in a comfortable chair or lying flat on her back on the floor. Tell her to close her eyes and to relax – you could read her a story to help her achieve this state. When you think she is quite relaxed, ask her to concentrate on how her arm and leg muscles feel, and to explain to you how they feel. She may say that they feel 'nice' or 'light' or 'warm'. Second, tell her to tense up her arm and leg muscles as tightly as she can, as though she is trying to grab hold of something with her fingers and toes. While she does this, ask her to explain to you what her arm and leg muscles feel like now. Discuss with her the difference between the feelings of relaxation and the feelings of tension. Drawing her attention to this difference in sensations may help her achieve a state of relaxation more easily in future. Explain that when she meets someone for the first time she should try to make her muscles 'nice' or 'light' or 'warm' (that is, the words that she used to describe them when she was feeling relaxed).

Relaxation also depends on the rate of breathing. A child who is tense will increase the rate of her breathing, while at the same time decreasing the amount of air drawn in with each breath. In other words, her breathing becomes rapid and shallow. This physical reaction reduces the amount of oxygen absorbed by the bloodstream, which in turn increases her anxiety further. So the management of breathing is very important in relaxation techniques. Suggest to your child that when she feels nervous she should try to slow down the speed at which she breathes. Slow deep breaths are best – after three of these she should then try to breathe at her normal, unexcited rate for a few minutes. This technique should be repeated until she calms down.

A child who uses all these techniques to communicate non-verbally that she is socially confident and relaxed will create an excellent first impression, and that will start any new relationship off on a positive footing. All it takes is practice from your child and encouragement from you. You'll both be surprised how easy it is to use body language effectively in this way, to your child's advantage.

Getting On with Others

Once initial impressions have been formed and children start playing together, there is the opportunity for true friendships to develop. Of course, friendships in childhood are often volatile – your child might be 'best friends' with a child one day and then have a completely different so-called 'best friend' the next. However, some friendships are more long-lasting; a lot depends on the emotional maturity and personalities of the children concerned.

Children also vary in their popularity. One child could be liked by lots of her peers, while another child could be isolated or even rejected. In many instances there is nothing that can be done about this because popularity in childhood often depends on a number of fixed physical attributes, such as a child's sporting ability and physical attractiveness – these qualities are hard to change. Similarly, popular children tend to be more intelligent. Yet you can help increase your child's popularity and her ability to keep and maintain friendships by paying attention to her body language, because psychological research has revealed a number of body-language features which make others feel comfortable. A child who transmits these non-verbal messages is more likely to get on well with her peers.

The dimensions of body language that have already been identified as central to creating a positive first impression are also important for maintaining childhood friendships – that is, good body posture, strong eye-contact, a smiling facial expression, and staying relaxed. Your child should always be encouraged to think about these aspects of her body language. But once friendships have formed, other features come into the picture.

Everybody wants to be listened to when they speak. Think about how you feel when you talk to someone – whether your partner or child – and then realize that they are not paying attention. You almost certainly feel annoyed, perhaps hurt that they are showing such little interest. Children feel that way too. That's why you should develop your child's **attentiveness** towards others who speak to her. Attentiveness has a number of components, the first of which is eye-contact. But it is not just about making steady eye-contact – that can also appear insincere and convey an underlying attitude of indifference. The eye-contact should be occasional and regular, not constant. At no time during the other child's talking should the listener allow her gaze to linger on anyone or anything for more than a second or two, otherwise it looks as though her attention has wandered aimlessly through boredom.

The child's facial expression should also be varied and appropriate. A would-be listener who smiles when she is being told a sad story or who looks depressed when hearing a pleasing tale is clearly not listening attentively. A completely blank expression can also convey the same impression. So the mood of the listener's facial expression should match the mood of the speaker's. Your child probably does this spontaneously anyway, but it is worth pointing out to her.

Research has also proved that a child is more popular when she gives **positive reinforcement** to her friends, by showing approval of their speech and actions. A smile when her friend gives her one of her sweets, an enthusiastic look on her face when her friend shows off a new toy, or a 'thumbs up' gesture when her friend manages to climb over an obstacle independently, are examples of positive reinforcement. In fact, any look or gesture that signifies approval comes into this category.

Young children (especially if they are less than 4 or 5 years old) are by nature egocentric and have difficulty thinking about other people's feelings. Therefore, they do not spontaneously transmit positive reinforcement through body language as frequently as adults – to do so requires a more mature sensitivity. Yet it is very effective in strengthening emotional ties between friends, and is a skill that your child could learn with your guidance and support.

The final aspect of body language to consider in this context are **pacifying gestures**. Watch your child and her friends playing together and you'll soon realize that the gestures they make towards each other can be aggressive or pacifying. The aggressive ones are obvious, such as snatching a toy out of another child's hands, scowling furiously at the others when things don't go according to plan, or even simply hitting out in temper. Everyone on the receiving end of these gestures knows what they mean, and they are given with the deliberate intention of conveying that emotion.

Pacifying gestures are more subtle but have equal impact on friendships. These gestures all imply an attitude of caring, not rejection, of security, not hostility; they are peaceful and friendly. Pacifying gestures usually involve hand movements, such as:

– clapping. This is a universal sign of approval. Every child is delighted to have her achievements applauded. Of course, it should be done infrequently or else it won't appear genuine, but an occasional short round of applause is always welcome as a recognition of achievement and approval.

– helping. In virtually every culture, an open hand usually signifies peace, while a closed hand signifies aggression. So a child who literally helps her friend by extending an open hand towards her, for instance to help pull her up from the floor, or to pat her gently on the back, demonstrates her friendship through body language.

– sharing. There is no better way to prove friendship than to share possessions; this is one of the most primitive ways of saying 'I like you and I want you to have what I have.' Unfortunately, children do not as a rule share instinctively; they have to be taught and shown how.

Teaching Positive Body Language – Do's and Don'ts

When trying to teach your child how to use non-verbal communication positively in order to enhance her relationships with other children and adults, the following guidelines may be helpful.

Do

Keep it fun. If you make it serious then both you and your child will become anxious. She won't learn anything if the atmosphere is tense. Keep it pleasant and calm.

Teach her at the level she can understand. There is no point in explaining about non-verbal communication in the same way that you might to an adult.

Show your approval when she uses positive body language naturally in her everyday interactions. Point these out to her, and explain why you are pleased.

Don't

Show your disappointment if you find that your child doesn't learn the skills of body language you are trying to teach her. Children vary in their ability to learn.

Be surprised to find that, although she does what you tell her when practising positive body language at home, she forgets all about these skills when she is outside.

Rush her. Concentrate on one aspect of positive body language at a time; when your child seems confident about using it, you can then move on to the next.

Summary

As well as concentrating on your child's body language in order to understand her better, you can help her to use particular aspects of non-verbal communication in a positive way to strengthen her friendships and popularity with other children. First impressions matter, and there is a lot your child can do with her body language to make those first few moments work in her favour, such as keeping up strong eye-contact, maintaining good posture and having a relaxed attitude. When it comes to your child's existing friendships, you can help teach her to be more attentive, to give appropriate approval to her friends, and to develop more sociable gestures. These techniques are all useful for enabling your child to establish and use positive body language.

Index

Of further interest…

Starting School

A parent's guide to preparing your child for school

Richard Woolfson

Starting school is a big step in any child's life and naturally every parent wants to give their child a head start so that his or her potential is fully maximised.

Starting School is a practical, accessible and reassuring guide for parents to help them prepare their child and themselves for that first day at school. It covers pre-school to the first year at infant school, including how to choose the right school for your child, pre-school learning, childhood development, the first day and what to do if things go wrong.

Your Child Can Be A Genius

Early learning through play

Ken Adams

Early learning can be creative and fun and will help pre-school children get the best possible start in education. This tried and tested home-learning programme is full of easy ideas and activities to encourage children to develop their natural talents without pressure and to stimulate an enthusiasm for learning which will help them throughout their school years.

Ken Adams is not only a parent, he is a teacher too. His creative teaching methods and his innate belief that every child has a natural ability to succeed first came to public attention when his son, John, passed his maths 'A' level at the age of nine. Now he shares, in clear terms and with appealing images, his home-learning plan which will help every parent to ensure that their child can make the very best of their natural talents.

Good Habits, Bad Habits

Dr John Pearce

Habits such as sniffing and thumb-sucking can provoke strong reactions in parents. Parents can also feel guilty and wonder if they are somehow responsible for their child's bad habit, or whether the habit is an indication that something is wrong.

Other habits are an important part of everyday life: getting up in the morning, dressing, eating meals, going to bed at night and so on are all routines that are repeated day in and day out so that they become unconscious habits.

Good Habits, Bad Habits tells you how children's habits are formed and why some children are more likely to develop habits than others. The simple guidelines in this book will help you to develop your child's good habits and deal with the so called bad ones that can cause you and your child so much embarrassment and distress.

Dr John Pearce has over 20 year's experience as a child psychiatrist.

Growth and Development

Dr John Pearce

All parents are interested in their child's emotional, physical and intellectual development.

Growth and Development outlines the stages your child will go through, to reassure and help you to understand your child's unique progress from birth to adolescence. Taking a look at what influences individual child development, this book covers a wide range of experiences, including:

the first years of life – developing self-awareness and self-esteem
the school years – learning how to relate to others, understanding abstract concepts and creative and artistic ability
adolescence – learning to cope emotionally and physically with approaching adulthood

In addition to the main stages of development, John Pearce provides information on problem areas such as reading difficulties or bedwetting which may be causing concern.

Fighting, Teasing and Bullying

Dr John Pearce

There are few things more frightening to a child than being the victim of bullying, whether by adults or other children – but many go on for months, suffering in silence.

If your child is a victim of bullying, or finds it difficult to control his or her own aggressive behaviour, John Pearce's book will help you to recognise this and offers useful strategies to help your child to learn self-control, develop confidence and improve self-esteem.

He explains:

the differences between fighting, teasing and bullying
how to tell when your child is being bullied – and what to do about it
strategies to help your child to cope
how to 'toughen up' your child for teasing
what to do if your child teases, fights or is a bully
how to cope with bullying in the family
when to worry about siblings fighting – and how to help your children be happy

Bad Behaviour, Tantrums and Tempers

Dr John Pearce

If your little darling has become a little horror, Dr John Pearce could hold the key to happier parenting:

Bad behaviour:

what makes a child naughty?
how can you teach your child good from bad?
what are the best methods of discipline?
what is the best way to deal with swearing, lying or hyperactivity?

Tantrums and tempers:

how can you help your child cope with aggression?
what can you do when you get angry?
how to cope if a child holds its breath or sulks
how to avoid the things that cause tantrums

Here are simple, practical and realistic solutions to common problems based on years of experience. Whether your child is two, a teenager or somewhere in between, you'll find something to help you in this book.

STARTING SCHOOL	0 7225 3100 1	£4.99	☐
YOUR CHILD CAN BE A GENIUS	0 7225 3116 8	£4.99	☐
GOOD HABITS, BAD HABITS	0 7225 2296 7	£4.99	☐
GROWTH AND DEVELOPMENT	0 7225 1724 6	£4.99	☐
FIGHTING, TEASING AND BULLYING	0 7225 1722 X	£3.99	☐
BAD BEHAVIOUR, TANTRUMS AND TEMPERS	0 7225 2818 3	£4.99	☐

All these books are available from your local bookseller or can be ordered direct from the publishers.

To order direct just tick the titles you want and fill in the form below:

Name: _____

Address: _____

_____

_____

_____ Postcode: _____

Send to Thorsons Mail Order, Dept 3, HarperCollins*Publishers*, Westerhill Road, Bishopbriggs, Glasgow G64 2QT.
Please enclose a cheque or postal order or your authority to debit your Visa/Access account —

Credit card no: _____

Expiry date: _____

Signature: _____

— up to the value of the cover price plus:
UK & BFPO: Add £1.00 for the first book and 25p for each additional book ordered.
Overseas orders including Eire: Please add £2.95 service charge.
Books will be sent by surface mail but quotes for airmail dispatches will be given on request.

24-HOUR TELEPHONE ORDERING SERVICE FOR ACCESS/VISA CARDHOLDERS — TEL: 0141 772 2281.